BUILDING A LEGACY

EDMONTON'S ARCHITECTURAL HISTORY

Edited by Allan Shute
Designed and typeset by Jamie Olson
Printed and bound in Canada by Friesens

Library and Archives Canada Cataloguing in Publication

Tingley, Kenneth W. (Kenneth Wayne), 1947-
Building a legacy: Edmonton's architectural history / Ken Tingley; photographs by Lawrence Herzog.
Includes index.
Issued also in electronic format.

ISBN 978-1-55050-545-0

1. Architecture--Alberta--Edmonton--History. 2. City planning--Alberta--Edmonton--History.
3. Edmonton (Alta.)--Buildings, structures, etc.--History. I. Herzog, Lawrence II. Title.
NA747.E3T548 2012   720.9712'334   C2012-906151-4

10 9 8 7 6 5 4 3 2 1

2517 Victoria Avenue
Regina, Saskatchewan
Canada   S4P 0T2
www.coteaubooks.com

Available in Canada from:

Publishers Group Canada
2440 Viking Way
Richmond, BC, Canada   V6V 1N2

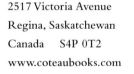

Coteau Books gratefully acknowledges the financial support of its publishing program by: the Saskatchewan Arts Board, the Canada Council for the Arts, the Government of Canada through the Canada Book Fund and the City of Regina Arts Commission.

KEN TINGLEY
PHOTOGRAPHS BY LAWRENCE HERZOG

BUILDING A LEGACY
EDMONTON'S ARCHITECTURAL HISTORY

CONTENTS

GREETINGS FROM THE MAYOR

The City of Edmonton is proud to celebrate and preserve its heritage, arts and culture. Heritage and interesting architecture are two ingredients that when combined, create memorable places – places people want to visit, where they want to do business and live.

Renewal and preservation are the keys to building great places in Alberta's capital city. Historic resources of all kinds link to our past and give citizens insight into the growth and development of Edmonton from a small prairie town to one of Canada's fastest-growing cities.

As our city grows, new dynamic projects are being built that in time will add to, complement and enhance the architecture of the past, creating a richer and more diverse urban landscape.

This book speaks to Edmonton's commitments to its varied architectural legacies. We salute the past city councillors, city builders and citizens who have contributed to what we have – and those who will follow, building on that foundation.

Edmontonians can be proud of how the city has grown and visitors can marvel at the legacies we have built and preserved over time.

Stephen Mandel

▲ 2A ▲ 2B

ACKNOWLEDGEMENTS

The City of Edmonton thanks the Alberta Heritage Foundation for its generous financial assistance, the consultants Ken Tingley and Lawrence Herzog whose words and images create this valuable history, and Coteau Books for its careful production. Many thanks are also due to the City of Edmonton Archives and the Provincial Archives of Alberta for the use of their historic images.

Also appreciated is the City's heritage and urban design staff of the Sustainable Development Department, past and present, who had the idea for an accessible, ordered record of the city's built history, and who also helped to develop its format and realize its final production. In particular David Holdsworth and Robert Geldart, the heritage planners, for managing the process, as well as Kulbir Singh, the former director of the group.

This book is a long-overdue tribute to all Edmonton's municipal politicians, the Edmonton and District Historical Society, the former Society for the Preservation of Architectural Resources of Edmonton (SPARE), the Old Strathcona Foundation, the Edmonton Historical Board, the Alberta Heritage Foundation, the architects, builders and all the citizens of Edmonton for their endeavours to build and preserve this city's heritage.

▲ 3A

▲ 3B

INTRODUCTION

This book highlights many of Edmonton's buildings that have been protected by the City of Edmonton or the Province of Alberta. It also seeks to provide historical context for the buildings, when they were being constructed. The buildings shown represent a broad range of architectural types, from grander buildings to modest residential structures, and reflect a cross-section of the many Edmontonians who contributed to our city's built heritage. The buildings described do not include all the significant resources in the city, but provide a good indication of those officially protected. Hopefully, many more will follow in the coming years.

At the turn of the twentieth century, early buildings were often boom-town style and were of simple timber construction. With the arrival of the railway, other building materials became more readily accessible and grander buildings more common. Brick construction became standard for more valuable commercial buildings, primarily to adhere to fire codes. Edmonton's most active period of building occurred after the Victorian era, when highly ornate structures were the order of the day. The Edwardian era buildings that represent the major pre-war boom in Edmonton continued the classical proportions and traditional detailing, albeit more modestly.

Subsequent building booms resulted in newer neighbourhood developments taking on the styles of their time, from catalogue homes and Craftsman influences, to postwar bungalows. It is easy to pass through various neighbourhoods and determine approximately when they were developed by their prevalent building types, adding another visible layer to our city's historic built fabric over time.

The book attempts to place structures in the appropriate decades they were built. Since most designated heritage structures represent the pre-First World War period, a conscious effort was made to distribute their descriptions throughout the book either where they could be relevant to another decade or purely for readability purposes.

FOREWORD

As a result of the destruction of many of the city's historic resources in the late 1970s and early 1980s, the City's then Planning Department became active in raising awareness about our city's heritage, including supporting publications such as The Lost Heritage of Edmonton and The Threatened Heritage of Edmonton in 1982.

In 1988, Edmonton City Council approved a heritage preservation policy and program with an annual incentives budget to preserve historic buildings. Shortly afterwards, the Inventory and Register of Historical Resources in Edmonton was created, recognizing over 400 buildings. Despite some hard economic times, the various City of Edmonton councils continued to support the Historic Resources Management Program and, as a result, Edmonton today has the largest number of designated

◀ *Connaught Armoury* 4A

The idea of a book on the preserved heritage of Edmonton has been in the minds of the heritage planners and urban designers since a major heritage inventory was conducted in the early 1990s.

properties in Alberta. The City's investment in heritage has seen significant economic, social and physical returns; and the award-winning heritage program is seen as one of the more successful in the country.

The purpose of this book is to highlight a variety of buildings or structures that have been restored and protected through the City's heritage program in partnership with their owners. They represent some of the best structures that remain and the more modest everyday buildings that represented buildings of the time, typical to the period that most people would have encountered.

This book covers the notable decades, providing insight into major events and influences upon them, such as wars, the Great Depression, floods and other disasters, booms and busts, immigration, building codes, bylaw annexations, sports,

education, and arts and entertainment. The impact of all these on the city's heritage has been tremendous.

In 1914 the author of *Edmonton: Alberta's Capital City* reminded its readers that Edmonton has been spoken of as a city "with no past, some present and an illimitable future." Today, as this book eloquently describes, we have a past, an energetic present, but still an illimitable future as long as we make wise choices in preserving and incorporating our built heritage to develop an environment that enriches our lives with beautiful architecture, art and culture. Many readers in the Edmonton region will recognize Ken Tingley as a well-known historian who has researched scores of heritage projects and authored many local historical books. Similarly, writer and photographer Lawrence Herzog has been closely associated with historical

architecture societies in Edmonton and is a regular contributor of articles on historical buildings in the Edmonton media.

Together, their work brings to life the history of Edmonton with over one hundred years of architectural heritage.

Ossama Elgalali RPP MCIP
Director, Urban Design Section
Sustainable Development
Department
City of Edmonton

THE LAND, THE RIVER, THE PEOPLE

The Ice Age created the river, and the river created the city.

Eighteen thousand years ago, the last great ice age was at its peak. The place where the City of Edmonton would stand millennia in the future was under an immense grinding ice sheet.

When the planet warmed and the massive ice tiers gradually withdrew, meltwater trapped by the retreating eastern glaciers could not follow its natural drainage, and the vast Glacial Lake Edmonton was created. This inland sea covered the region until it burst out of its restraining

◄ *As a result of a farsighted City of Edmonton policy to purchase lands along the river for park purposes, the North Saskatchewan River valley is the largest urban park in North America. Edmonton's downtown lends a crowning touch to the Capital City Recreation Park which maintains a sense of the wild in the heart of a 21st-century metropolis.* 6A

moraine to the south about twelve thousand years ago, allowing the great primordial North Saskatchewan River to carve its path to Hudson Bay over the newly drained plains and marshlands.

The North Saskatchewan River has changed continuously since then, beginning with a relatively rapid deepening of the valley after the drainage of Glacial Lake Edmonton. The river cut down through the deep moraine for several thousand years until it hit impermeable clay-covered bedrock. Prevented from carving the channel deeper, the river began digging into the valley walls. For centuries it ground out the soft sediments, sculpting the deep escarpments and forcing its way through different channels with each massive seasonal runoff or powerful flood. The river has scoured out the valley on many occasions, washing away familiar features and depositing others.

By the time human habitation began, the river had broadly assumed its present course, and by the seventeenth century, it marked the meeting place of plains and parkland. Soon it would also mark the northern boundary of a violently contested strip of land stretching south to the Battle River where the Cree from the north and Blackfoot from the south were the principal combatants.

The people of the First Nations used the North Saskatchewan River valley and its sheltered terraces for millennia before the first Europeans arrived. Four or five deeply buried occupations, probably campsites, were recently identified in Rossdale in soils laid down above and below a layer of volcanic ash known as the Mazama Ash. This easily recognizable layer of grey ash was deposited sixty-eight hundred years ago when the mountain occupying the

▲ 8A

site of today's Crater Lake in southern Oregon exploded and blanketed the region in volcanic dust. Pre-Mazama occupations, the first human habitation identified along the North Saskatchewan River, lie about three metres below the present surface of the land. Post-Mazama occupations are associated with two layers of buried soils located above the ash layer, where archaeologists have recovered butchered bison and other animal bones, as well as stone tools. Two radiocarbon dates on bone recovered in 1999 from the lower of these occupations in Rossdale indicate an age of about fifty-five hundred years.

Stratified campsites such as those identified at the Rossdale Site are extremely rare in the North Saskatchewan River valley and other valleys in the Central Alberta Parkland, although similar early occupations appear more frequently along the Bow and Oldman rivers to the south. The

Rossdale Site suggests a very long use of the river flats by the First Nations within the present city of Edmonton. Archaeologists believe the occupations may have been sporadic, resulting in a diffuse scatter of artifacts across the site.

The North Saskatchewan River flats provided First Nations with convenient camping spots and protection from seasonal fires sweeping across the plains to its southern bank. Vast herds of bison migrated here. Beaver, muskrat and deer were abundant. Plains grizzlies and wolves hunted the great elk herds grazing on the plains. Though flood deposits from periodic inundation during the nineteenth century cover most recent aboriginal activities, there is some evidence that First Nations were still using the valley flats up to the arrival of the fur traders at the end of the eighteenth century.

Teepees, sometimes called lodges at the time, were the principal dwelling of the First Nations people who visited the river valley. Teepees provided shelter, warmth and protection from the elements; and despite their simple appearance, they evolved over thousands of years to withstand extreme weather conditions, ranging from the intense heat and violent storms of summer to the bitter cold and heavy snows of winter.

A deceptively simple-looking assembly, the teepee was a conical tent often covered with skin. It was a light and portable dwelling that evolved to meet the special needs of the nomadic people of the plains and parklands, most of whom had to be mobile as they followed the seasonal movements of bison herds and other food sources.

The teepee consisted of a set of ten to fifteen sapling poles (usually of the appropriately named lodgepole pine), an outer skin

covering, an inner skin lining and a skin door. The real brilliance of the teepee lay in its smoke flaps at the top, which allowed for cooking over an open fire, and its inner lining, which directed a steady and controllable flow of fresh air even as the sun pounded down or the blizzards howled outside. The lodgepoles additionally served as the frame for a dog travois, and later horse travois, used to transport possessions from one location to the next.

In most Plains cultures, most of which were matrilineal, the teepee belonged to the women of the family, who would raise, dismantle and maintain it, and who were able to expel a husband if they wished. When camp was made, the women first unloaded the travois and tied together three lodgepoles at what would be the teepee's upper end. This tripod was then put up to form a triangle on the ground with the lashing rope left long enough to

▲ *Canvas or skins were wrapped around lodge poles to create the distinctive and exceptionally functional teepee, and were used and seen well into the twentieth century.* 9A

wrap several times around the tripod and hang almost to the ground. About a dozen more poles were added to this frame, their upper ends resting against the tied apex of the cone and their lower ends forming a circle spaced around the triangle frame. The lashing rope was wrapped around the top of the poles three times and pulled tight, tying the added poles to the crown of the teepee. The outer skin was tied on a pole, raised to the teepee top and wrapped around the frame. The overlapping seam was closed with smooth, sharp lacing pins, and the door was attached to one of the lower pins. The base was pegged to the ground, and the free poles were adjusted to provide the right tension in the outer skin. A cord was strung from pole to pole in the interior

▲ *Teepees and tents could still be seen in Rossdale in 1920, but such impermanent dwellings were giving way to newer structures that were being built in the city.* 9B

at head height to receive the inner lining. Two long poles used to adjust airflow were attached to the smoke flaps at the apex. They were usually set at right angles to the prevailing wind to draw smoke out of the teepee. Air flowed over the top edge of the liner and down to the floor before being drawn up again by the heat of the fire.

At times, teepee camps were the largest communities along the North Saskatchewan River, especially during buffalo hunts.

After the arrival of European fur traders, First Nations gathered in large numbers at the river to trade at the Hudson's Bay Company's Fort Edmonton and the North West Company's Fort Augustus.

Though such camps were regular occurrences, they were always a matter of tension and excitement. On one occasion an important visitor recorded the events. Sir George Simpson, the "Little Governor" of Rupert's Land, had begun a famous voyage around the world in August 1841. As the new representative of the Hudson's Bay Company, he wished to survey his empire, which covered over one-third of modern-day Canada, an area so vast that it had not yet been adequately explored or mapped. The traders kept a wary eye on a visiting First Nations' village that suddenly appeared on the flats to the south, across the river from Fort Edmonton. In the early morning, the Blackfoot camp awoke, smoke began to rise from the lodges, dogs barked, horses nickered and women gathered at the riverside to get water for the morning meal. Soon hundreds of men, women and children were walking among the teepees, stretching, calling to one another and planning the day's events.

▲ *Teepees remained a part of the river valley scene as late as the 1920s. McKay Avenue School can be seen on the river escarpment, a sign of changing times.* 10A

On his third day at Fort Edmonton, Simpson recorded that the early morning was marked by the firing of guns in the First Nations' encampment. Nine chiefs representing the Blackfoot, Peigan, Sarcee and Blood "all dressed in their grandest clothes and decorated with scalp locks,"

▲ *Sir George Simpson in 1857, some time after his round-the-world tour.* 11A

▲ *A Teepee added symbolic significance to the banquet celebrating the new City of Edmonton* 11B

asked to be conveyed across the river to the fort. Simpson noted in his account that some three hundred and fifty teepees finally formed the camp on the south bank of the river. Such a camp could represent over a thousand people. The teepee retained an ambiguous symbolic value throughout early European settlement in the Northwest Territories. When Edmonton was incorporated as a city in October 1904, the celebratory banquet held at the Thistle Rink included a teepee as part of the decorations. For some it may have added an interesting historical adornment to the festival atmosphere or represented a lament for a passing way of life.

EUROPEANS STAKE A CLAIM 1795-1870

Anthony Henday was the first fur-trade explorer the Hudson's Bay Company sent as far west as present-day Edmonton to establish new trading opportunities.

The First Nations people he met in this land of mighty rivers, sweeping plains and shining mountains possessed a culture that allowed them to survive in what was an alien land to Henday, and he relied upon them as he moved deeper into the country. His arrival heralded a period of western exploration during the next century that saw great change for aboriginal peoples. Following in Henday's footsteps, the great mapmakers and traders Peter Pond, David Thompson and Alexander Mackenzie left their indelible marks on the future of what was then the Northwest Territories, a vast area stretching from present-day

◀ *Canada's foremost 19th-century painter and ethnographer Paul Kane captured this evocative scene of Fort Edmonton in the mid-1800s during his western tour to visit the First Nations people and their landscapes before they were forever altered by encroaching Europeanization.* 12A

northern Quebec and Ontario through the Prairies to British Columbia and north to the Arctic Ocean. The booming trade in beaver pelts brought many Europeans who cast their futures in the new land.

By the turn of the eighteenth century, the fur trade companies directed and controlled development of the Northwest, and the commercial partnership between First Nations and European traders was strengthened. The rich trapping grounds of the Beaver Hills, located about fifty kilometres east of the present site of Edmonton, gave its name to Beaver Hills House, or *amisk wuche waskahegan* in the Cree language, the first name by which European settlement near Edmonton became known. The Cree became the primary aboriginal group along the North Saskatchewan River by the late eighteenth century when the first fur posts were being

built in what would become Alberta a century later. The future of the Cree from this point onward was tied closely to the fate of the European fur trade as the buffalo were hunted to virtual extinction and Plains people's nomadic life following the herds became ever more difficult to maintain.

The Métis, a unique western Canadian people, arose from the first contact between the European newcomers and the First Nations. Many traders married aboriginal women, who then filled an essential role in the fur trade, becoming full trading partners and undertaking much of the arduous work necessary to survive in a harsh wilderness. The Métis took an active and indispensable role in exploring, trading, freighting furs, buffalo hunting and general commerce of the plains and parklands. By 1885 about a thousand Métis lived in the Edmonton area.

By the early 1880s, four European fur trading posts were located in or near the North Saskatchewan River flats below present-day Edmonton in the district now known as Rossdale. The Hudson's Bay Company's Edmonton House II and the North West Company's second Fort Augustus were established around 1801–02. Both companies would construct new forts in the Rossdale Flats between 1813 and 1830.

After 1830, when the final Fort Edmonton was moved to a higher location safe from the ravages of regular flooding, the river flats were used for a variety of purposes. Native camps on the low ground below and east of Fort Edmonton were common, and the area was probably cultivated on a small scale.

When artist Paul Kane visited Fort Edmonton in 1846, he painted the Hudson's Bay Company's impressive fortification

▲ *The Boat Brigade Leaving Fort Edmonton for York Factory, 1825, a painting by J. D. Kelly in the Confederation Life Collection, depicts the excitement as the York boats begin the long journey to Hudson Bay* 14A

on the river heights below the present site of the Legislature Building. The "Big House," a three-storey log edifice within the high stockade, was famed as the administrative and social centre of the vast

◄ *Métis citizens were influential in the political, social, and cultural life of early Edmonton. Laurent Garneau, one such individual, is pictured here with his wife, Eleanor. Garneau gave his name to the residential area surrounding the University of Alberta. His famous fiddle, which led the music at many social gatherings, is on the table at his side.* 15A

construction. Hip or gable roofs and sash windows thus characterized the Company's forts in the Northwest. This basic style was used across Canada, but as Wade indicates, it was not a national style, but rather a style associated with the fur trade era.

A post-and-sill method of wood construction was used by the Hudson's Bay Company for most nineteenth-century structures. The use of vertical corner posts is basic to all types of horizontal even-tier construction, including post-and-sill. Four types of such corner-post construction have been identified. The first consists of vertical posts with continuous grooves into which the tapered ends of the horizontal logs are placed. In the second, typical of most Hudson's Bay Company buildings, the vertical posts are mortised into a sill and the tapered ends of the horizontal logs are slid into place between grooved uprights. A third uses four posts driven

Northwest Territories. Workshops, clerks' and married men's quarters, a chapel and the interpreters' cabin and trade house, with carefully restricted access through a separate palisaded entrance, also were located within the stockade. Four imposing blockhouses commanded a view of the river valley and the immediate trading area, as well as the favoured aboriginal campsites on the flats and opposite bank of the river. A lookout tower increased the

security of the fortress. Nearby stood a windmill used to grind flour for the local inhabitants. During the 1840s, the fort was a hive of activity, bustling with trade and the constant work on the York boats that transported the furs to market in the East.

Historian Jill Wade observes that factors' memories of houses of eighteenth-century lairds in Scotland influenced the Hudson's Bay Company's building design and

into the ground so that the horizontal logs are held more firmly in place between the uprights. A fourth method consists of a "hog and trough" of planks, the apex set into the corner with wings abutting the ends of the horizontal logs, to which they are either spiked or pegged.

Yet another identifiable characteristic of post-and-sill construction is the use of

several minor vertical uprights. It was not uncommon for a building to have from five to ten uprights on one facing. This not only added to the strength of the building, but also permitted the use of shorter logs while placing no restriction on the size of the structure. When doors or windows were added, they were usually set between the minor uprights or beside one of the major uprights.

▲ *An early colour postcard, circa 1911, of the old Hudson's Bay Company buildings at Fort Edmonton clearly illustrates the post-and-sill construction technique used in most Hudson's Bay Company posts.* 16A

European commerce in the Northwest Territories paved the way for settlement that accelerated the rate of change facing the indigenous peoples of Western

Canada. The Hudson's Bay Company exercised its hegemony over a virtual western empire until the decline of the fur trade and the emergence of the new Dominion of Canada. Canada purchased this vast territory and soon it would be incorporated within the National Policy, which envisioned the development of the Northwest Territories, coupled with the construction of a transcontinental railway and the industrial development of Central Canada.

These profound changes heralded a radically new direction for the Northwest, and the First Nations and Métis would suffer from the dislocations attending the widespread and fundamental changes in their lives that followed the disappearance of the old fur trade empire and decline of the buffalo.

▲ *The final Fort Edmonton in 1912. Three years later, a great flood washed away much of the development in the flats below, such as John Walter's mill on the opposite bank of the river. While the fort survived, it was dismantled to make way for progress in 1915.* 17A

EDMONTON'S FIRST URBAN GROWTH
1870-1904

Edmonton sprang up almost overnight along the banks of the North Saskatchewan River. The world had responded to news of the "Last Best West" in Western Canada, where plenty of cheap land was available despite the closing of the official American frontier in 1890.

Settlers, entrepreneurs and land speculators flooded in. The Edmonton district was rapidly transformed by a succession of events beginning with the arrival of the first Christian missionaries in 1840, who would assume de facto administration of the vast Northwest and introduce the controversial residential school system to accelerate the rate of aboriginal assimilation.

Next the North-West Mounted Police came to Fort Saskatchewan in 1874, bringing European law and order to the Prairies, followed by the arrival of the Calgary and Edmonton Railway, which connected the Canadian Pacific Railway's main transcontinental line at Calgary with the

◄ *John Walter's City of Edmonton steaming past Gallagher's Flats in about 1915. The flats were later named Cloverdale for early prospector Tom Clover.* 18A

new village of South Edmonton in 1891. When the first federal land survey was completed in 1882, this established the grid through which European settlement would be managed. While missionaries and Mounties were harbingers of the abrupt cultural transition that would descend on the Northwest between 1870 and 1885, the railways and land survey would transform the land physically between 1885 and the turn of the century.

Where the railways went, settlement followed, and the land soon was occupied and homesteaded. In 1869 the new Dominion of Canada paid the Hudson's Bay Company £300,000 to surrender its 1670 royal charter over Rupert's Land and the Northwest Territories. The Hudson's Bay Company retained 20 per cent of the arable land in the territory, making it the largest private landowner in Canada.

The federal government moved swiftly to impose order in its new lands by dispatching the Northwest Mounted Police, who arrived at Fort Saskatchewan in 1874. Between 1876 and 1899 treaties were made with the First Nations to establish rights to settlement in the territories. The arrival of the European rule of law established a framework for property ownership, allowing the first settlers to begin acquiring and developing property.

In 1882 and again in 1912, the Hudson's Bay Company divested itself of some of its lands around Edmonton in the "greatest land sale in history." At the same time, the federal government offered virtually free land to homesteaders who would "prove up" their claims by breaking land, cultivating some of it and building a "soddie" or shack. Western European and Scandinavian immigration arrived in waves, most arriving

▲ *South Edmonton sprang up at the end-of-steel in 1891. The Dominion Hotel and the Douglas, Ross, Baalim, and Malone business blocks located along a muddy Whyte Avenue in about 1900, before the radial railway tracks were laid.* 20A

▲ *Land buyers taking a bet on the future of Edmonton throng 103 Street during the Hudson's Bay Company land sale on May 13, 1912.* 20B

in the Edmonton district aboard the Calgary and Edmonton Railway. The population of the Northwest Territories swelled from under 60,000 to over 200,000 between 1881 and 1901, and grew at an even faster pace in the years preceding the First World War.

In Edmonton the first lots to be surveyed and sold were long, narrow strips of land stretching from the riverbank to the heights above, conforming to practices common before the Dominion Lands Survey. These river lots followed a tradition established along the river systems of New France and served a similar purpose in giving settlers access to the basic resources they needed

to survive: water, flat farmland and a ready supply of wood. This also allowed homes to be built fairly close together, which provided security and encouraged community spirit. The lasting legacy of this system can still be detected on the north side, where it is reflected in the angled street patterns located east of 97th Street, from the McCauley-Boyle neighbourhoods as far as the Highlands. After fur, the second natural resource to attract people to the banks of the North Saskatchewan was gold. Between 1860 and 1907, thousands of ounces of gold were dredged or panned from the river gravels. In 1898 Edmonton became a staging point for the Klondike Gold Rush, profiting from its questionable championing of the arduous and sometimes deadly "All Canadian Route" to the northern gold fields.

One of the region's first entrepreneurs, John Walter, arrived at Fort Edmonton in 1870. Born in the Orkneys in 1849, he

was highly valued by the Hudson's Bay Company for his traditional Orcadian skill as a boat builder. Within five years he had saved enough money to buy River Lot 9, located on the south bank of the North Saskatchewan River, on which to pursue his fortune.

In 1875, Walter built a house – the first to be constructed on the south side of the river – with logs taken from Whitemud Creek and Big Island. This house was briefly Edmonton's first telegraph office, headquarters for the ferry captain, a small general store and a stopping house for travellers. During the Northwest Rebellion of 1885, frightened residents took refuge behind the stout log walls of the Walter house.

Walter constructed the grandly named cable ferry, Belle of Edmonton, which replaced the oar-powered scow that had previously been the only transportation across the river. Walter's new craft could carry six loaded carts and their draft animals. John Walter prospered through his entrepreneurial spirit, quickly becoming a part of what Edmonton historian J. G. Macgregor called an "aristocracy of accomplishment." Walter built a second house next to the first during 1885–86. Diversification into coal mining and lumber milling soon made Walter a millionaire, and during the Klondike Gold Rush in 1898, he moved his first home to where it now stands and began building a larger third dwelling. Constructed of spruce, poplar and birch, and insulated with wood shavings from his mill, it was one of the largest houses in the city when it was finished in 1901.

In 1907 the riverside neighbourhood

▲ *The Treaty Commission gathers on May 29, 1899, near the first Alberta Hotel in preparation for leaving Edmonton to negotiate Treaty Eight.* 21A

known as Walter's Flats was officially renamed Walterdale in his honour, but by then the years of Walter's good fortune were drawing to a close. The Low Level Bridge – constructed 1899–1900 with the 1902 addition of the grandly named Edmonton, Yukon and Pacific Railway, which carried freight a short way into the northwest of the city – began to replace John Walter's ferries as the preferred means of delivering goods. In 1913, with the completion of the High Level Bridge, Walter's heyday as a ferry operator came to an end. A year later the 105th Street Bridge, now called the Walterdale Bridge, opened.

Walter turned to the construction of the steamboats City of Strathcona and City

▲ *A large gold dredge works the gravel bars on the North Saskatchewan around 1900.* 21B

of Edmonton, named for the twin cities sprouting up on opposite sides of the river. For years, excursions on Walter's steamboats took happy Edmonton picnickers and holiday celebrants upstream to Big Island for memorable festivities. But, in June 1915, a record flood destroyed much of the industrial heart of Edmonton's river flats, carrying away the brickyards, dairies and other manufacturing plants, along with Walter's lumber mill. Walterdale resident Norman Guild recalled Walter walking back and forth, repeating over and over again in his Scottish burr, "It'll nae come o'er the banks." When it did, sweeping away all his dreams, Walter was ruined. To compound his misery, his bookkeeper absconded with $50,000. John Walter died on Christmas Day 1920. It was a sad end to an energetic and important

life, one that personified the cycles of boom and bust that would characterize the growth of the city in the years to come.

The "Twin Cities" of Edmonton and Strathcona mushroomed on both sides of the river following the election of the Wilfrid Laurier government in Ottawa in 1896. The village of South Edmonton was established at the northern end of the Calgary and Edmonton Railway in 1891, and quickly grew into the town of Strathcona in 1899. By 1907, Strathcona was proclaimed a city. Edmonton, a town by 1892, had already become a city in 1904. The rivalry between these two cities, sometimes good-natured and sometimes more heated, reached a peak between 1907 and 1912, when the two were amalgamated. Under Clifford Sifton and Frank Oliver, Laurier's ministers of the Interior, great efforts were made to develop the Northwest through railway building and massive immigration. The influx of settlers spurred the rapid settlement of agricultural land around Edmonton and a frenzied burst of urban development on both sides of the river. At first, Edmonton was a horse-powered city. The delivery of ice, water, coal, milk and other goods relied on thousands of dependable teams cramming the streets and an army of boisterous teamsters who

▲ *Onlookers watch the flood of 1899 inundate the power plant across the river. The flood of 1899 proved a blessing in disguise for the builders of the Low Level Bridge when it demonstrated that the planned supports for the bridge were not high enough to survive the highest floods. C.E. Tighe took this photograph at the bridge site on 18 August 1899.* 22A

delivered the goods demanded every day by a young city bursting at the seams. As a new century approached, Edmonton and Strathcona seemed poised for even greater progress. Men and women from Central and Eastern Canada, the United States, the British Isles, Ukraine and other European

▲ *In 1908 a mighty Reeves steam traction engine hauls a small house down 101 Street to a new location, making room for another, undoubtedly larger home.* 23A

▶ *Teamsters on McDougall Hill delivering goods from the railways to the city centre just before the First World War. The Legislature Building, Donald Ross's Edmonton Hotel, and Diamond Park can be seen in the distance.* 23B

countries were rushing to a land with their eyes fixed optimistically on the promise of limitless opportunity. For another decade these dreams would be thoroughly realized.

Strathcona Hotel

Constructed 1891
10302 82nd Avenue
Designated Municipal Historic
Resource May 2007

The Strathcona Hotel is significant for its association with the development of South Edmonton and the Town and City of Strathcona, as well as its simple frontier design. The Strathcona Hotel is a three-storey commercial structure with a hipped roof, clapboard siding and a corner entrance. It is located on the northwest corner of Whyte Avenue and Gateway Boulevard in the Old Strathcona Provincial Historic Area.

The hotel was built in 1891 as a railroad hotel for the Calgary and Edmonton Railway Company, across the street from the railway station at the "end of steel". The Strathcona Hotel was the first hotel in South Edmonton (renamed the Town of Strathcona in 1899) and thus served as a stopping point for immigrants seeking to establish homesteads or businesses in the Northwest. From 1891 to 1904, it was the largest hotel in the region with 45 guest rooms. Because it relied heavily on revenue from the tavern located in the west annex, prohibition in 1916 forced the sale of the hotel. It was purchased by the Presbyterian Church, who used the building to house the Westminster Ladies College from 1918 until the year after the repeal of prohibition in 1923, when it reverted to use as a hotel.

▲   24A

Built in 1891, with subsequent additions in 1903 and 1907, rendering an unusual L-shaped floor plan, with two annexes, the Strathcona Hotel is the oldest wood frame commercial structure in Edmonton. Typical of frontier buildings, little consideration was given to exterior ornamentation, and in this case it is the large hipped roof, the brackets under the eaves, and the pediments over the windows and doors that give the hotel any design distinction it may possess as a late Victorian commercial architectural building.

▲ 25A   ▲ 25B

John Walter Houses

Constructed 1875, 1886 and 1901
9180 Walterdale Hill
Designated Municipal Historic
Resource August 2004

The John Walter Houses are associated with one of the most important early Edmonton businessmen and community builders. These three dwellings were successively built and occupied by John Walter (1859–1920), the first person to settle permanently on the south bank of the North Saskatchewan River within Edmonton.

The three houses as a unit reflect the

Walter family's growing prosperity and the different facets of their family life. The first house is a simple timber, hewn-log structure built in 1875; the second, another hewn-log structure, built in 1884, is larger and accommodated his growing family; and the third, built in 1901, exhibits Queen Anne Revival characteristics.

Walter built the first cable ferry west of Winnipeg to connect the north and south sides of the river, and started Edmonton's first industry here as a boat and cutter builder. He then established Edmonton's largest sawmill and became known as Edmonton's "first millionaire" before losing

his fortune to the flood of 1915, which destroyed his mills and facilities. His wife, Annie Newby, continued to live in the third house until her death in 1942 and made a distinctive mark on its appearance.

The John Walter Museum and Historic Area provides rich evidence of the evolution of building techniques during the earliest years of Edmonton's history, from the most rustic of shelters to more refined and genteel accommodation. The log structures were built with readily available materials, and worked on site with little refinement, a reflection of the rough frontier conditions and isolation of the settlement. The 1901

▲ 26A ▲ 26B

house demonstrates the rapid evolution
of the local construction industry and the
new availability of manufactured building
materials. Milled lumber and lathe-turned
decorative components demonstrate a
sophisticated and progressive attitude,
and illustrate the rapid maturation of
the settlement. These buildings provide
valuable physical information about
the history of local construction.

Orange Hall

Constructed 1903
10335 84th Avenue
Designated Municipal Historic
Resource May 2005

The Loyal Orange Hall #1654 is tucked inconspicuously into a corner of 84th Avenue and the lane located behind the Old Strathcona Public Library. It still sits in its original location and continues to have presence and importance for the people of Edmonton despite being hemmed in by the Arts Barns and the library. The Orange Hall is one of the oldest-surviving public assembly buildings in Alberta and played an important role in the early settlement and cultural life of Strathcona when it was still a separate city.

The Orange Hall is a simple wood-frame building with a plain clapboard exterior and a high-pitched gable roof, a significant example of vernacular frontier construction typical of utilitarian building methods at the turn of the twentieth century. Historical photographs indicate that the white clapboard siding originally was painted a dark colour; the enclosed front porch is a later addition. However, it remains much as it was originally constructed over a century ago. The assembly hall has been used mostly for concerts since the 1970s and features hardwood flooring, wood wainscotting and a stage with a centre podium, with a carved wooden arch. Lodge

▲ 27A

members built the hall themselves to save on labour costs, while the interior was plastered and painted for all of $240.

The Loyal Orange Lodge in Strathcona was formed in 1895, with the first meetings held in the home of the founding member and treasurer H. W. Nash, a Strathcona grain buyer. Robert McKernan, owner of the Dominion Hotel, organized several Orangemen's parades and was subsequently grand master of the lodge. Every year on the "Glorious 12th of July" the members of the Orange Lodge would parade down Whyte Avenue in honour of William of Orange, a Protestant who became King of England in place of James II, a

Catholic. The first parade was held in 1895, composed of 60 Orangemen and a fife-and-drum corps. By 1904 the group's membership had grown considerably; an impressive 2,500 Orangemen from all over Alberta participated in that year's procession. Originally a partisan group supporting the cause of Protestantism in England, today Strathcona's Orange Hall operates primarily as a benevolent association, raising funds for various children's charities. The hall frequently hosts musical and dramatic events, and craft sales.

▲ 28A

Pendennis Hotel
Constructed 1904, Renovated 1912
9660 Jasper Avenue
Designated Municipal Historic
Resource July 2001

The Lodge Hotel is a good surviving example of the early Edwardian classical design frequently evident in the commercial blocks of the early twentieth century. The original west wing is a relatively rare survivor of a wood-frame commercial building, while the east wing is a comparatively early example of a structural steel frame. Its façade is an early example of the Edwardian Beaux Arts influences gaining popularity in brick commercial buildings of the time. The Lodge Hotel is an important component of the Jasper East Block north of Jasper Avenue and east of 97th Street. The Jasper East Block, developed during Edmonton's last major pre-war economic boom of 1908–12, is one of the few remaining contiguous period streetscapes in Edmonton.

Originally opened as the Pendennis Hotel in August 1904, the establishment featured a parlour, tavern, office, large and small dining rooms, and bedrooms on the second and third floors. Until the 1920s the Pendennis Hotel was a popular dining spot as well as a hotel. "The table is admittedly one of the best in this city," claimed the Edmonton Bulletin in 1913. A menu for Christmas dinner included twelve courses for fifty cents.

Nathan Bell purchased the Pendennis in November 1905. Bell had lived in Winnipeg and then Calgary, where

he worked in the cigar-manufacturing business while his brother ran a hotel in the city. Nat Bell then operated a successful hostelry, the Bell Hotel, in Dawson. With the revenues from that business, Bell was able to purchase the Pendennis.

The Edmonton office of the Calgary architectural firm Lang, Major and Company was retained to design an addition in 1912. The principals of the firm – George Macdonald Lang and William Paul Major – resided in Calgary. The new addition contained many modern conveniences, including hot and cold water, electric lights, steam heat and electric-bell communication within the building.

Prohibition in 1916 forced the hotel into a period of decline, and in 1920 it fell into bankruptcy and was later converted into a rooming house. In 1945 it was renamed the Kenmo Lodge Hotel, a contraction of the names Kennedy and Mogen, the new owners.

John Toma, another new owner, shortened the name to the Lodge Hotel in 1981. More recently, this restored building

▲ *Early image of the Brighton Block and the Pendennis Hotel on Jasper Avenue.* 29A

has been taken over by the Ukrainian-Canadian Archives and Museum of Alberta to retain and display its holdings.

A NEW CITY FOR A NEW CENTURY
1904-1913

Jasper Ave Looking West. Edmonton Canada.

McCutchon Studios. No 6

The years between 1904 and 1913 brought two bursts of exceptional growth interrupted only by an economic downturn in 1907.

Edmonton was transformed in every way during this decade as the population grew almost nine times from 8,350 in 1904 to 72,500 by 1913. By comparison, the entire Northwest Territories comprised 79,300 inhabitants in 1901.

In this decade a series of amalgamations had expanded the boundaries of Greater Edmonton, culminating in its union with the City of Strathcona in 1912.

Real estate speculations and the development of the University of Alberta would drive the proliferation of subdivisions that almost, but not quite, filled in the

◀ *"With unpredcedented population growth and rapid development, Edmonton was quickly transformed from a city of wood to one of stone and brick and a major urban centre."* 30A

boundaries. Many new Edmontonians hailed from Ontario or the British Isles. This common background influenced their choice of architecture; and much of the development during the early part of the century was consequently based on the English styles with which they were familiar and with which they associated success and prestige. New railways linking Edmonton with outside markets sped up the financial growth; new bridges such as the High Level Bridge drew the community closer together, both socially and commercially. The result was a spurt of growth that truly changed the city forever.

Edmonton became a city on October 8, 1904. As in all cities of the era, the first streets, rail lines, bridges and public buildings were largely hand built through the muscle and sweat of thousands of workers. Between 1904

and the Great War of 1914–18, the city's core would be transformed from a city of wood to a city of brick.

The local and regional workforce ebbed and flowed with the seasonal demands of construction and railway building, as well as the lumber camps and mines. While mechanization played an increasing role in the rate at which the city was evolving at this time, what really drove the change was a twofold impulse to make the city safer from "the fire demon" that regularly destroyed small-town wood-framed buildings, and the desire to create grander structures reminiscent of those in the hometowns of its community builders, many of them from Ontario and Eastern Canada.

On September 1, 1905, the Province of Alberta was proclaimed, and the following year Edmonton was confirmed as its capital.

That August, C. E. MacPherson, the general passenger agent for the Canadian Pacific Railway, visited the city to arrange single-rate fares from all over the province to Edmonton for the inauguration ceremonies.

A great deal of heated debate had centred on whether the capital of Alberta should be located at Edmonton or Calgary. The rivalry between the two cities dated back to the 1880s when the Canadian Pacific Railway chose the southern city for its route across Western Canada. Frank Oliver, the federal government's new minister of the Interior and a native Edmontonian, became Edmonton's foremost champion. In May 1906 his newspaper, the Edmonton Bulletin, printed a large map of Alberta with Edmonton at its centre. "Where Should the Capital Be?" queried the caption. The creatively designed map left little doubt in the minds of Edmontonians at least. Calgarians

▲ *A view northeast toward McDougall Hill from McKay Avenue School in about 1905.* 32A

disagreed, but Edmonton emerged the victor in the second Battle of Alberta.

On March 15, 1906, the first session of the provincial legislature convened at the Thistle Rink because the young province did not yet have a permanent legislature building. Two months later, legislative sessions were moved to the upper floor of McKay Avenue School, a more distinguished brick structure. Today that chamber has been recreated as it looked in 1906 at McKay Avenue School.

Less than three months later, on November 24, the last spike for the Canadian Northern Railway was driven in the city, providing Edmonton with an independent transcontinental rail connection to domestic and international markets. From 1891 to 1905, the city had been dependent upon

▲ *This view east from the top of McKay Avenue School demonstrates how the city core was becoming transformed into impressive clusters of brick structures by 1913. McDougall Methodist Church, All Saints Anglican Church, the Court House, and the Revillon Brothers Building can be seen.* 32B

the Calgary and Edmonton Railway and its little connector line, the Edmonton, Yukon and Pacific Railway. A second railway, the Grand Trunk Pacific, arrived in 1909, and by 1915 the railway had opened its landmark Hotel Macdonald.

Speculative land transactions and development close to stations, yards and other facilities were typical of western Canadian urban expansion during the heyday of railway construction. Every town seemed to have its "Railway Street" lined with warehouses, stores and grain elevators.

OPENING OF ALBERTA'S
FIRST LEGISLATURE
EDMONTON MAR.15.190
PHOTO COPYRIGHT B

In the larger centres such as Strathcona and Edmonton, residential neighbourhoods and commercial districts were generated in an almost predictably uniform pattern. Like rivers, railways shaped the communities that clustered along their lines and rambling routes.

In 1908 the University of Alberta opened in Strathcona. When Strathcona amalgamated with Edmonton in 1912, Edmonton inherited that city's title of the province's "university city." The new century celebrated and embraced new technologies. Joe Morris brought the first automobile to the city in 1904. That same year, Edmonton established the first municipally owned telephone system in Canada. Automatic telephone service was launched in 1908, another first in Canada, and the Edmonton Radial Railway became the most northerly streetcar system in North America. Pilot Reginald Hunt amazed Edmontonians

▲ *Edmonton was largely a hand-built city raised up through the sweat and muscle of men like these workers in 1910.* 33A

when, on Labour Day 1909, he flew his experimental flying machine on the first powered flight in Western Canada. In February 1911, Bessie Nichols became the first woman to win an election in Alberta when she became a school trustee.

A new modern century was opening up with seemingly limitless possibilities, and Edmonton felt part of it. In the eventful year of 1912, Edmonton amalgamated with Strathcona, and the Hudson's Bay Company held its second big land sale, attracting long queues of excited speculators.

This tremendous land sale opened up the area between Namayo Avenue (97th Street) and 122nd Street to new residential development. The old Company continued

▲ *The first Alberta legislative session was held at the Thistle Rink, the only building in the new capital large enough for the occasion at the time.* 33B

to shape the destiny of Edmonton in this way long after the grip of ownership had slipped from its hand. Ironically, much of the land was not developed until decades later due to a market crash. This explains why the communities between Westmount and McCauley are not as old and have significantly fewer older properties than their adjacent neighbourhoods. In that same year, Annie Jackson became the first female police officer several years before women could vote in provincial or federal elections. The year in many ways marked the high point of exuberant growth and boundless ambition before the First World War.

Edmonton's Warehouse District was at the commercial heart of the city during its formative years before the war. The district bustled noisily day and night with trains, horse teams and trucks transferring goods from the railway spurs that interpenetrated its many warehouses. This was the real entrepôt of the north in its heyday, when Revillon Frères and the Hudson's Bay Company supplied the advancing northern resource frontier. Existing structures such as the Metals Building and the Canadian Consolidated Rubber Company warehouse are a reminder of those days and form the core of the area now known as the historic warehouse district.

MAGOON AND MACDONALD LEFT THEIR MARK

Herbert Alton Magoon (1863–1941) and George Heath MacDonald (1883–1961) were the principals of the architectural firm of Magoon and MacDonald. Magoon was born and educated in Quebec but received his architectural training in Chicago. He first practised in Iowa, Illinois and Nova Scotia. MacDonald was born in Prince Edward Island and began his architectural career in the Montreal offices of Percy Erskine Nobbs and Edward, and then W. S. Maxwell, before working with his uncles as a contractor.

Magoon and MacDonald met while working at the Dominion Iron and Steel Company in Sydney, Nova Scotia, where Magoon was employed as an architect and MacDonald as a draftsman. They moved to Edmonton in 1904 and set up practice with MacDonald as Magoon's assistant. MacDonald returned to Eastern Canada to finish his education, graduating from McGill University in 1911 with a bachelor's degree in architecture. The two became partners and practised together from 1912 until Magoon's death in 1941.

Among their many quality designs were the McDougall Methodist Church (1909–10), the Tegler Building (1911, demolished 1982), Old St. Stephen's College (1911), the Public Library (1923, demolished

1968), the Salvation Army Citadel (1925), and the T. Eaton Company Mail Order Building (1929, demolished 1983). MacDonald continued the practice after Magoon's death and was one of the first to show an interest in reconstructing Fort Edmonton, about which he wrote a book.

▼ *McDougall Methodist Church. 34A*

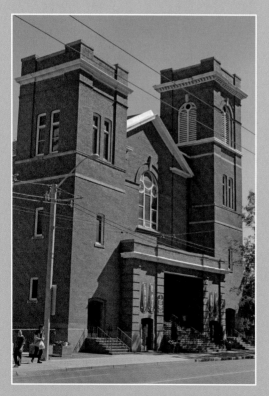

FIRST. MAYOR AND COUNCIL. 1905.

▲ *Early City councillors: (back to front and left to right) William A Griesbach, Kenneth McLeod, James Henry Hargreaves, Chas May, G. J. Kinnaird, K. W. McKenzie, W. H. Clark, J. R. Boyle, Joseph Henri Picard and D. R. Fraser.* 35A

▼ *Main Street in Strathcona on August 11, 1912, just after the vote to amalgamate with Edmonton gives evidence the forerunner to 104th Street still turned to mud following a good rain, although the sidewalks and newly planted boulevard saplings promised greater things.* 35B

▲ *Members of the Builders Exchange meet in the King Edward Hotel for their annual banquet in 1910. This thriving group is represented in the front row by Mayor George Armstrong, right foreground, and busy contractors Charles Batson and C. R. Frost on the left.* 35C

◄ *Completion of the first direct transcontinental rail link for Edmonton is celebrated at the Canadian Northern Railway depot in Edmonton in 1905.* 36A

◄ *This view of the Warehouse District in 1913 includes Ross Brothers, Ames Holden and an A. Macdonald warehouse. The stately Tegler Building can be seen in the distance.* 36B

▲ 37A

McKay Avenue School
Constructed 1905, Renovated 1912
10425 99th Avenue
Designated a Provincial Historic
Resource May 1976 and June 2000

McKay Avenue School replaced the original Edmonton School erected on the same site in 1881. It was named in honour of Dr. William MacKay, a physician for the Hudson's Bay Company from 1864 until 1898 and one of the earliest doctors in Western Canada. The name of the school (and the avenue on which it is located) was incorrectly written McKay in later years and this misspelling remains in use.

In 1904 Governor General Lord Minto laid the cornerstone for the new building that would exemplify the Richardsonian Romanesque style in Edmonton with its red-brick façade, rough-faced sandstone string coursing, arched windows and doors, and recessed main entrances with Ionic columns. Designed by Henry Denny Johnson, the architect for the Edmonton Exhibition Building (1901) and the Imperial Bank in Strathcona (1902), McKay Avenue School became a model for later school buildings in the city. An addition was added in 1912 to meet the needs of the city's growing population.

In 1906–1907, sessions of the Alberta Legislative Assembly were held on the third floor of the school after the first gathering in the Thistle Rink. During these two working sessions, the legislation to establish the infrastructure of the new province was crafted. Many significant decisions were made in the McKay Avenue School, such as the confirmation of Edmonton as the provincial capital, the founding of the University of Alberta in Strathcona and the creation of the provincial court system.

The original 1881 schoolhouse, being the first free public school in Alberta, was restored as an Edmonton Public Schools centennial project in 1982 and moved up from its river valley location to within a few hundred metres of its original location. Its new urban park and landscaped setting allows appropriate interpretation of the site's history, while providing an opportunity for people to enjoy a green open space on the valley edge in the urban setting.

Canadian Pacific Railway Station

Constructed 1907
8101 Gateway Boulevard
Designated Municipal Historic
Resource November 2003
Designated Provincial Historic
Resource December 2004

In 1890, construction began in Calgary on the Calgary and Edmonton Railway under contract for the Canadian Pacific Railway. When the "end of steel" terminus was established on the south side of the North Saskatchewan River, the community of South Edmonton was created, which would become the town of Strathcona in 1899 and a separate city in 1907 before being amalgamated with Edmonton in 1912. End of Steel Park commemorates the fact at the northern end of Gateway Boulevard (103rd Street).

The first train arrived in South Edmonton in the summer of 1891. End of steel would remain south of the river until the Low Level Bridge was completed in 1902, allowing the Edmonton, Yukon and Pacific Railway, an affiliate of the Canadian Northern Railway, to link the town of Edmonton to the railway network. The first railway station was inadequate for the massive influx of settlers during the pre-First

World War boom, and in 1907 the present station was constructed. In the same year, Strathcona became a city, and the grand new station signalled the achievement of both the Canadian Pacific Railway and the city fathers of Strathcona. The station was built in keeping with the chateau style favoured by CPR President William Cornelius Van Horne for the railway's hotels and stations. Inspired by the chateaux of the Loire region of France, the more simple brick façades were enhanced by the distinctive French-inspired flare of the rooflines that became so familiar a sight in Canadian cities.

An addition was built onto the south in a style replicating the original architecture. Eventually CPR moved its operations south of the existing site into a new building, again of a sympathetic design. CPR sold the original station to commercial interests that now operate restaurants and taverns.

▲   38A

◀   38B

Margaret Martin Residence

Constructed circa 1907
8324 106th Street
Designated Municipal Historic
Resource April 2005

The Margaret Martin Residence is a two-and-one-half-storey brick-clad house with a wraparound veranda located at the corner of 84th Avenue and 106th Street in the Strathcona neighbourhood. The house was one of the first to be built in West Strathcona, one of two areas into which Strathcona was originally divided. To the west of 99th Street, residents were largely business people; to the east, residents were generally tradespeople or Canadian Pacific Railway and Gainers employees. A few of the grand residences and institutions survive, including the nearby Bard Residence and the Strathcona Collegiate Institute, built in 1907.

Margaret and David Martin were Strathcona pioneers. After spending some time farming in the Dakotas – as did fellow Strathconians such as the Ritchies, McDonalds and Gainers – the Martins acquired in 1899 a large tract of farmland in what is now called the Pleasantview neighbourhood. Shortly after their arrival in Strathcona, their young daughter died of pneumonia. Most burial sites at the time were near Whyte Avenue, but David Martin knew that when spring came, coffins often washed out of the

▲ 39A

ground. He buried his daughter on his new farm, where he also soon would be buried. The site became the Mount Pleasant Cemetery, the first consecrated municipal graveyard on the south side of the river.

Martin died a year after his daughter, but his wife stayed on the land with their eleven children. Another daughter, Grace Martin McEachern, became a well-known teacher, for whom an Edmonton school was named in 1972. As the population in the area grew, the farm was subdivided and became known as the Martin Estate until the 1950s, when it became Pleasantview. The grand house was completed around 1907, the year Strathcona grew to city status. The Martin Residence is significant as an example of the popular foursquare style and one of the few built in brick. It remains an early surviving example of the work of the Magoon, Hopkins and James architectural partnership,

which later was counted among the most respected architectural firms in Western Canada. Magoon, Hopkins and James were among the best architects attracted to Edmonton's booming construction industry after Alberta became a province. Herbert Alton Magoon (1863–1941) arrived in Edmonton in 1905, the same year that Edward Colis Hopkins (1857–1941) was appointed provincial architect. English born and trained, P. Leonard James (1878–1970) arrived in Edmonton in 1906, and during his two-year stay won the competition for the Strathcona and Royal Alexandra hospitals, and completed a number of other significant projects. In 1908 James relocated to British Columbia, where he became one of the province's most prominent architects.

The Margaret Martin Residence is one of the few buildings to survive from his short-lived partnership with Magoon and Hopkins.

▲ 40A

brick detail, including regularly spaced piers, corbelled brick dentils under the cornice, arcaded detailing, voussoir lintels with recessed window bays between the piers, arched windows with stone sills, recessed rough brick panels between windows set in a stacked header bond, and a raised stone parapet.

The Jasper Block was designed by Hopkins and Wright, who also were responsible for the Horne and Pitfield Building (10301 104th Street) and the Great West Saddlery Building (10137 104th Street).

The Jasper Block was developed by John Kelly, who was working as a blacksmith in 1902, but who, by the end of the decade, had made the leap into real estate development by establishing Owner's Realty. Kelly also built the Kelly Block on what today is Rice Howard Way. Kelly left Edmonton in the early 1920s for California.

The building's interior was completely rebuilt to accommodate new uses, parking and another floor, while retaining its historic shell and character.

Jasper Block
Constructed 1909
10514–10520 Jasper Avenue
Designated Municipal Historic
Resource May 2004

The Jasper Block is an example of the turn-of-the-century commercial architecture that once had a strong presence in downtown Edmonton. The building had space for commercial outlets at the street level and apartments above, as well as an unusual recessed light well to illuminate the rooms above the first floor and a central skylight to bring natural light into the central hall.

The south façade, facing Jasper Avenue, exhibits its original 1909 face with

North-West Trust Building
(Union Bank of Canada)
Constructed 1910–11
10053 Jasper Avenue
Designated Municipal Historic
Resource August 1996

The ornate North-West Trust Building, located on the south side of Jasper Avenue between 100th and 101st Streets, was at the heart of the emerging commercial district, where many banks established their presence. In 1870 the Union Bank, established by its Quebec parent company in Lethbridge, became the first bank in the part of the Northwest Territories that would become Alberta 25 years later. The Union Bank opened an Edmonton branch in 1901, and by 1910 required a new office. The Union Bank was later acquired by the Royal Bank of Canada.

The Union Bank occupied the Jasper Avenue premises from 1911 until 1927 with the offices on the upper floors leased to various tenants. James Richardson and Company purchased the building in 1928 for their grain trading and stock brokerage. Richardson continued to lease office space on the upper floors. From 1970 the building was the head office of the North-West Trust Company, which purchased the building in 1979. Today it plays a role in the thriving life of Jasper Avenue as a boutique hotel and restaurant.

◀ 41A

◀ *The new Union Bank Building brought classical elegance to Jasper Avenue in 1911. Real estate offices springing up like mushrooms reflected the building boom that characterized Edmonton before the First World War.* 42A

The North-West Trust Building design reserves its primary architectural statement for the main Jasper Avenue façade, for which architect Roland Lines created an impressive Renaissance-inspired composition with some Baroque detail expressed in local pressed red brick and white Bedford limestone from Indiana. The combination of contrasting brick and stone is associated with the earlier English Renaissance tradition and belongs to the renewed Renaissance Revival style that appeared as a late phase of Edwardian Classicism. Edmonton newspapers described the building at the time of construction as "Modern Renaissance."

The ground floor is a rusticated stone-clad base bearing a massive order of six Ionic pilasters climbing to the third storey and culminating in an entablature with a bracketed cornice. Arched windows show Baroque influence, as does the entrance portico. Paired rusticated Tuscan columns raised on pedestals originally supported an entablature crowned by a broken segmented pediment rising to the sills of the second-storey windows. The pediment carried the carved coat of arms of the Union Bank. These features did not survive changes to the ground floor windows and entrance.

Before dying in action in 1916 while serving with the First Field Company, Canadian Engineers, architect Roland Lines left several signature buildings in Edmonton, including the Alex Taylor School (1908), the Norwood School (1909), Strathcona Collegiate Institute (1909), the Looby Block (1909), the Canada Permanent Building (1910), the original Royal Alexandra Hospital (1911), the Exhibition Stock Pavilion (1914), and the Lac La Biche Inn (1916, destroyed by fire 1989). The vacant bank was restored and converted into a boutique hotel in the 1980s, with a significant addition to the rear. The historic building's prominence on Jasper Avenue was enhanced by subsequent Rice Howard Way and public art improvements by the City which provided physical improvements to the east of it.

LeMarchand Mansion

Constructed 1910–11
11523–11525 100th Avenue
Designated Provincial Historic
Resource July 1977

LeMarchand Mansion, situated in the
Oliver district overlooking the North
Saskatchewan River, is an H-shaped
apartment designed by leading local
architect A. M. Calderon. An architectural
gem of its type, it exhibits its Beaux
Arts influences through a brick façade
and sandstone window details, cornice
and columns. A three-storey span of
windows capped by an arch gives the
western façade an impressive aspect.
Attractive columns, pediments, arches and
voussoirs further accent this impression.
Wrought-iron balconies, a prominent
cornice and the central projection on
the north façade complete the effect.

LeMarchand Mansion featured fireplaces
and exterior windows in every suite,
Edmonton's first elevator and natural-gas
heating provided by a coal-degasifying plant
built on site. A fireplace with a gleaming
brass hood set into marble flooring in the
lobby made for an impressive entrance.

The building's first owner, René
LeMarchand, a Parisian in his 50s, arrived
in Edmonton in 1905, attracted

43A ▶

to the region by his brother Alphonse, a member of the Missionary Oblates of Mary Immaculate. Edmonton legend has it he had brought with him a sizeable cache of second-hand straight razors he had acquired from an eccentric Parisian nobleman who used each one just the once. This allowed LeMarchand to set up a luxury-goods store in Edmonton and enter into the booming real estate market of the day. He obtained investment capital from the Union Garcons de Café in France and began construction on LeMarchand Mansion. It opened in 1910 as one of the first major apartment blocks in Edmonton, although the west wing was not completed until a year later. LeMarchand Mansion would be

the address of many prominent lawyers, business people and doctors who found its location near the city core attractive, while politicians enjoyed its proximity to the site of the new Legislature Building.

In 1913 the *Edmonton Journal* published a special Christmas issue extolling the rapid growth of the city, in which apartment blocks were singled out for special attention: "Among the marked features of Edmonton's growth and development during the past two years is the large number of modern apartment houses that have gone up and the completeness with which they have been designed to meet the needs of a large and growing city.

As an illustration of how well apartment houses pay in Edmonton there is not one of these structures that is not giving a return of (less) than 10 per cent on the investment and in some instances as high as 30 per cent is earned."

Unfortunately, by 1913 the boom was over, and most apartments would not realize such profits for some time to come.

▲ 45A   ▲ 45B

Charles J. Carter Residence

Circa 1909
10002 107th Avenue
Designated Municipal Historic
Resource November 1997

The circa 1909 Carter Residence, named for its first occupant Charles J. Carter, is a typical single family residence of the time owned by Edmonton's entrepreneurs. The house is a rare instance of an inner city residence that has retained a strong relationship with an original outbuilding, in this case a horse stable. The Carter Residence and stable, although moved a short distance from its original location at 10002-107 Avenue in 1995, retains its significance as a neighbourhood landmark.

The large two-storey, wood frame, L-shaped house has a distinctive wrap around verandah with turned Doric columns . Notable wood trim detailing includes return eaves, a notable gable with decorative shingles and dentillated pattern below, corner boards, frieze boards and broad window trims.

The horse stable at the rear with its Dutch gabled roof and hayloft, was typical, with its traditional rectangular shape, wood frame construction, drop siding, regular window and structural openings, sliding door (east facade), a diamond shaped window above the loft entrance and projecting pulley beam.

Hugh Duncan Residence

Constructed 1911
8520 104th Street
Designated Municipal Historic
Resource April 2005

The Hugh Duncan Residence is a prominent
house located on the corner of 104th Street
and 86th Avenue in Old Strathcona. It
is an excellent example of the popular
Edwardian era foursquare style that is
characterized by its symmetry, generous
proportions, and restrained detailing. The
house was located in an affluent upper-
middle class neighbourhood, where the
social aspirations of prominent residents
were reflected through its formal and
classical revival stylistic elements.

Hugh Duncan was a pioneer pharmacist
in Strathcona who owned and operated
his Whyte Avenue Pharmacy for
many years. He lived in this house
from 1911 until his death in June of
1935. Among Duncan's achievements
were his election as Mayor, chairman of
the first Edmonton School Board, and
Member of the Legislative Assembly.

▲ 47A

High Level Bridge
Constructed 1910–13
109th Street & 98th–99th Avenues
Designated municipal historic site
September 1995

The High Level Bridge was constructed by the Canadian Pacific Railway, whose subsidiary line, the Calgary and Edmonton Railway, was the first to reach the Edmonton area. The construction of the bridge was a principal factor in the drive to amalgamate the twin cities of Edmonton and Strathcona.

This structure illustrates the importance of the railway in the early history of the city better than any other bridge or freestanding structure in Edmonton.

Construction commenced in 1910, and the first train chugged over the High Level in 1913, the year amalgamation came into effect.

The design is attributed to P.B. Motley, the CPR's Engineer of Bridges and a bridge designer of national importance. Other engineers associated with the design are J.E. Schwitzer of the CPR and G.E. Roehm and C.M. Goodrich of the Canadian Bridge Company. The bridge was constructed by the CPR Bridge Department, Montreal.

The bridge's reinforced concrete piers, steel legs on the Strathcona approach, and steel superstructure were characteristic of bridges of the time. Conventional truss designs were added for the reinforced concrete roadway for cars. In its early years, the High Level was the only bridge in Western Canada to accommodate trains, streetcars, automobiles, and pedestrians.

The High Level Bridge measures 777.2 metres long from back wall to back wall along the road deck, with the base of the rail deck elevated 47.5 metres above the mean water level. The bridge comprises twenty-eight spans, including three Pratt Truss spans over the river and two Warren Truss spans over the north approach.

City Council identified substantial rehabilitation work to be undertaken on the High Level Bridge commencing in 1995.

Because the Edmonton Radial Railway Society runs a trolley service from Oliver to Strathcona during the summer months, the High Level Bridge retains its function as a railway bridge. The trolley line was further enhanced by extending it further north, with more stops and knitting it to the 'Ribbon of Steel' Multi-modal Transportation Corridor. New landscaping along the rail line and a multi-use path create an attractive route away from the busier roads, and links Jasper Avenue to Ezio Farone Park on the river valley edge.

▲ *The High Level Bridge was reaching the end of its construction as the newly completed Legislature Building towers above remnants of old Fort Edmonton.* 48A

▶ *The old trolley line still runs over the High Level Bridge during the tourist season.* 48B

▲ 49A

Thomas Scott Residence
Constructed 1912
9938 85th Avenue
Designated Municipal Historic
Resource June 2000

The 1912 Thomas Scott Residence is
an excellent example of the Foursquare
style, which became popular during the
Edwardian Era. The simple foursquare
dwelling is typically a two-storey square
or rectangular building, having four rooms
on each level. The front was typically
symmetrical with a large veranda, hipped
roofs and some Craftsman style woodwork.
They were popular during this period
and now contribute significantly to the
characters of many mature neighbourhoods.

North Telephone Exchange Building

Constructed 1912
10105 112th Avenue
Designated Municipal Historic
Resource September 1999

Familiar to the many researchers who have visited the City Archives over the years, the North Telephone Exchange recalls the rapid advances made in communications technology before the First World War. New entry doors and a modern flat-roofed canopy were added at the north façade during the 1970s, providing a different main entry point to the building. The original main entrance was a single door at the east façade on 101st Street. Though these components have changed the original appearance and character of both elevations, evidence still remains of classical influence in the horizontal stone banding at the main floor, the projecting wraparound metal cornice at the second floor and the stone-capped, raised and segmented parapet walls at the east and west gable ends. The old Exchange is characterized by its symmetrical composition and large window openings, which allowed ample natural lighting and ventilation for workers and equipment. The North Telephone Exchange Building operated in its original capacity until 1958.

New interior partitions were added to both the basement and main floors as part of the Historical Exhibits Building conversion

▲ 50A

in 1960 and the City Archives renovations in 1974. A new stair was constructed at the north entry and a storage vault added.

In 1881 Alex Taylor launched Edmonton's first telephone exchange, a manual magnetic system that used a crank to signal an operator who completed the connection. By 1904 over 500 telephones were in service and a new system was needed. The City of Edmonton purchased Taylor's phone company that year to operate as a municipal

utility, and in 1908 the manual system was replaced with the Strowger automatic telephone system that was touted as the most modern and economical of its time. Many cities in Eastern Canada did not install automatic exchanges until the 1920s.

Two new telephone exchanges were constructed in Edmonton in 1912 in the north and west to serve the most rapidly growing districts. Allen Merrick Jeffers designed both buildings, with the

firm of Purcell and Foote receiving the contract for construction of the North Edmonton Telephone Exchange.

Jeffers received his training in architecture at the Rhode Island School of Design and in the Providence office of G. W. Cady and Sons, Architects. He arrived in Edmonton in 1907 and that same year was appointed provincial architect. In this role Jeffers designed the Alberta Legislature Building (1907–13), the Wetaskiwin Court House (1907), the Calgary Normal School (1908), Athabasca Hall at the University of Alberta (1911), and Government House (1913). Following his work for the Alberta government, Jeffers became the Edmonton Municipal Architect from 1912 to 1914. As city architect he designed a number of municipal buildings, including the Telephone Exchange Buildings, the Civic Block (1912, refaced 1962 to serve as the main police station, then demolished in 1995 to make way for the Winspear Centre which opened in 1997), and the Court House (1911, demolished 1972).

Jeffers became a member of the Alberta Association of Architects in 1914 and practised privately in Edmonton until moving to Prince Rupert in 1922 and then to Los Angeles in 1923. Jeffers' work on the Telephone Exchange Building shares many design and detailing similarities with the Wetaskiwin Provincial Court House.

First Presbyterian Church
Constructed 1911–12
10025 105th Street
Designated Provincial
Historic Resource September
1978 and June 2000

First Presbyterian Church was designed by the Strathcona architectural firm of Arthur G. Wilson and D. E. Herrald, who left their imprint on many early Strathcona buildings such as the Strathcona Public Library and Rutherford House.

Built in the Late-Gothic Revival Style of Redcliffe pressed brick with Bedford stone trim, First Presbyterian generally appears English-inspired while incorporating suggestions of more outspoken French-Gothic elements in the triple-arch motif of the main porch and the large pointed-arch windows on the sides and front façade. The tower features twenty tubular chimes, a gift in 1913 from John A. McDougall, a pioneer city businessman. The organ with oak case and mahogany console was built in 1909 by Casavant Frères of Saint-Hyacinthe, Quebec. The pulpit from the 1902 church is still in use.

Reverend Andrew Browning Baird established the First Presbyterian congregation in Edmonton in 1881,

◀ 52A

holding the first services in Reverend George McDougall's Methodist church.

The congregation then moved to a room above a downtown grain warehouse. A manse and wooden church opened in 1882, serving until 1902, when a brick church was built. The Reverend Baird

was succeeded as pastor in 1887 by the highly respected Reverend David George McQueen, who served the church for forty-one years. McQueen became the first moderator of the Alberta Synod of the Presbyterian Church and a moderator of the Presbyterian Church of Canada.

The colours of the 63rd Battalion, Canadian Expeditionary Force, were presented to McQueen in 1916, the same year his son Alex McQueen was killed in France. The colours remain in the church sanctuary.

Molstad Residence

Constructed 1912
9633 95th Avenue
Designated Municipal Historic
Resource March 1994
Designated Provincial Historic
Resource November 1996

The Molstad Residence, located on a corner lot on 95th Avenue, once known as Molstad Avenue, is a large brick-clad dwelling with cedar shingles. Although essentially a basic urban foursquare design, it was larger and more finely designed than most and used higher quality materials. The interior has been restored to the original plan as a single-family dwelling, although it was divided into apartments at one time.

The Molstad Residence was built for Edward and Addie Molstad as part of an estate that occupied five lots and once included expansive grounds and gardens, fountains, a circular drive, carriage house and servants' quarters. Molstad established the early and successful real estate companies of Molstad and Company Ltd., as well as Fort George and Fraser Valley Land Company.

◄ 54A

George Durrand Residence

Constructed circa 1912–13
10417 Saskatchewan Drive
Designated Municipal Historic
Resource April 2002

The Durrand Residence represents a typical brick dwelling built in the neoclassical Edwardian style. It is located on the south side of Saskatchewan Drive on the south escarpment of the North Saskatchewan River, facing the historic city core across the river. Saskatchewan Drive provided ideal lots for the homes of the emerging commercial and professional class in early Strathcona. When George Durrand decided to build a residence along Saskatchewan Avenue, as it then was named, a notable representation of influential community leaders had already constructed significant homes in the neighbourhood. The home remains intact except for a veranda, which has been removed. The Durrands, a large family of early contractors and teachers, lived here from 1913 to 1919.

The Durrand House, like many of the houses remaining along Saskatchewan Drive, is representative of a substantial type of domestic structure inhabited by the upper-middle class in the early twentieth century. Built by the owner to his own requirements, it displays the scale and presence necessary to fit into the genteel atmosphere created by the emerging commercial, cultural and political group that

▲ 55A

placed special demands on new construction. The house has generous proportions, and its attractive detail seems to take its cue from the homes around it. The house is solidly built, as would be expected from a family working in construction and carpentry.

The site remains part of a contiguous row of dwellings representative of the boom-time urban growth immediately preceding the pre-war commercial collapse of 1913 and the outbreak of the First World War.

Harold Macdonald also lived at this location from 1920 until 1923. In 1911 he formed the construction firm Reed, Macdonald and Brewster, and in 1918

launched H. G. Macdonald and Company. In 1947 he formed Christensen and Macdonald Ltd., which for many years had its offices in the Tegler Building. His companies built the Milner Building, the Edmonton Journal Building, All Saints Cathedral, Holy Trinity Church, the Royal Alexandra Hospital, St. Joseph's Cathedral, and many other schools and churches.

Charles S. Edwards lived at this location from 1923 until 1969. At the time of purchase, he was a teacher at Strathcona High School. Edwards came to Edmonton in 1912 and began teaching in 1913. He taught until his retirement in 1943.

▲ 56A

Sheriff Robertson Residence

Constructed 1913
8120 Jasper Avenue
Designated Provincial Historic
Resource May 1987

The Robertson Residence is one of the earliest Canadian adaptations of Frank Lloyd Wright's influential Prairie Style.

The style, named for a Wright design published in the *Ladies' Home Journal* in 1901, emerged in the early twentieth century in Chicago. Prairie houses were characterized by low-pitched roofs featuring wide overhanging eaves, a determined horizontality that brought them close to the earth, large hearths separating the living areas, the predominant use of natural building materials, and an emphasis on craftsmanship.

The Sheriff Robertson house, designed by architect Alfred Marigon Calderon, embodies all these elements and features a cross-shaped plan, a striking octagonal skylight and a porte cochère, permitting wheeled vehicles to enter from the street.

At the time of its construction in 1913, the Robertson house was one of the most architecturally notable constructions in Edmonton. The interior featured a baronial fireplace, Tiffany lamps and elegant wooden mouldings, trims and furnishings.

Walter Scott Robertson arrived in Edmonton from Eastern Canada in 1881 and established a general store. Like many other businessmen of the era, Robertson invested in the local real estate market. He was appointed deputy sheriff of the Edmonton District in 1884 and Sheriff in 1905. Sheriff Robertson was a patron of the arts, owning an opera house and supporting local cultural activities.

The year 1913 saw a severe collapse in the real estate and investment markets, but ironically also witnessed some of the most ambitious building projects in Edmonton. That year Robertson commissioned his magnificent retirement home overlooking the North Saskatchewan River. Sadly, he died in 1915. His family continued to live in the residence until 1919.

Gibson Block

Constructed 1913
9608 Jasper Avenue
Designated Municipal Historic
Resource May 1994
Designated Provincial Historic
Resource January 1995

The Gibson Block is a large wedge-shaped brick building occupying part of a triangular block on Jasper Avenue at the eastern edge of Edmonton's commercial core that flourished before the First World War.

The Gibson Block is a rare example of a commercial building in the Flatiron Style, so named for its distinctive triangular shape. The Flatiron design, which originated in New York in 1902, was popular in North American cities before the First World War as a practical and remunerative way of using oddly shaped parcels of real estate. The Gibson Block also incorporated elements of the Chicago Style with its vertical emphasis of pilasters and windows contrasting with a horizontal motif in continuous-glass shop fronts and cornices.

Developed by realtor William Gibson, an uncle of successful real estate entrepreneur W. J. Magrath, the building has mirrored the changing fortunes of the city's commercial district. Gibson commissioned architect A. W. Cowley to design a building based on the famous New York Flatiron model. J. Sheridan was the general contractor,

assisted by the prominent local firm of George Pheasey and Charles C. Batson. Gibson sold his interest in 1914, moving to his home in the Highlands and farming a property near Clover Bar. The Gibson Block originally housed retail space on the first floor, offices on the upper floors and Turkish baths in the basement. The upper floors were converted to apartments in 1914 by the new owners Paul Max Schubert and Max Wenzel, who renamed the building the Schubert-Wenzel Block. The name never stuck, perhaps because of anti-German sentiment occasioned by the First World War. The Gibson Café advertised in a sign painted on the west wall of the building that it employed "White Help Only". Through misguided efforts to sanitize our history, this revealing declaration was removed during the building's restoration.

The Gibson Block fell into considerable disrepair, and at the City's initiative it was purchased and then resold at a significant discount to the Edmonton City Centre Church Corporation, which along with other agencies completely restored and renovated the building back to its landmark status. Today the block serves Edmonton as the Women's Emergency Accommodation Centre.

▲ 57A

A. Macdonald Building

Constructed 1913–14
10128 105th Avenue
Designated Municipal Historic
Resource May 2000
Designated Provincial Historic
Resource May 2003

The A. Macdonald Building was built during the decline of the building boom that shaped Edmonton prior to the First World War. It served as an important part of the Warehouse District that supplied the needs of the city's growing population during its first five decades.

The conspicuous red-brick, four-storey building on the corner of 105th Avenue and 102nd Street has been a prominent landmark in the district north of the Canadian National Railway right of way since it was built.

The design of this building was one of the most distinguished among Edmonton's warehouses. Most buildings of this type were treated externally with a flush façade having windows "punched" in or with pier-and-spandrel articulation. Among the latter, the A. Macdonald Building was one of the tallest and most attractively designed. It was rivalled only by the design of the five-storey Great West Saddlery Building, which still stands on 104th Street. The exterior brick walls are set on a stone base. Typically a hard, red brick was used on the two principal elevations and a softer common brick, painted grey, on the other two. The walls, reflecting the internal post-and-beam system, are articulated by a pier-and-spandrel motif with vertical piers located between each pair of windows, evident on the south and west elevations, and coinciding with the structural bays. The spandrels between the rows of wooden sash windows are recessed behind the piers.

Above the fourth-storey windows, a row of brick corbels brings the window plane out to meet the piers, at which point there once was a strong cornice. A low peaked parapet rose behind the cornice and supported a flagpole. The windowless east elevation is brick and serves as a base for a large painted wall sign. The west elevation has four arched truck-loading bays.

The two front bays on the ground floor contained offices. The different use is indicated externally by windows without brick mullion separations and with smaller upper sashes with entablatures above them. A classical entablature supported by four rusticated pilasters frames the entrance. Alterations have hardly changed the original appearance.

A. Macdonald Company, H. H. Cooper and Company, Macdonald-Cooper Ltd., and Macdonald's Consolidated Limited have all operated out of this building over the years. The Winnipeg-based A. Macdonald Company also had branches in Kenora, Saskatoon, Moose Jaw, Lethbridge, Fernie, Nelson and Vancouver. All these companies were represented by Harry H. Cooper, who came to Edmonton from Winnipeg in 1904 to be manager of the A. Macdonald Company's Edmonton branch. He established himself as a leading member of the Edmonton business community, serving as president of the Board of Trade and the Chamber of Commerce.

▲   60A

Holy Trinity Anglican Church

Constructed 1913
10037 84th Avenue
Designated Provincial Historic
Resource April 1983

Holy Trinity Anglican Church is a substantial steel-frame building that is most immediately conspicuous for its distinctive clinker-brick cladding. Built in the Gothic Revival style, Holy Trinity is marked by a square crenellated front tower and prominent stained-glass windows. The adjacent parish hall, added in 1949, is pleasingly sympathetic in its massing and materials. Holy Trinity Anglican parish was established in 1893 when only seventy-five

people lived in the settlement of South Edmonton, later to become Strathcona. Parishioners built a little frame church on the corner of 81st Avenue and 100th Street. Before this, Church of England worshippers gathered in the first Calgary and Edmonton Railway station and later in the little one-room school. In the manner of the time, the first church was moved to another lot in 1900, where, in 1906, a basement was excavated for the present church.

When the financial crisis of 1907 hit, the faithful were forced to worship in the basement of the uncompleted church. The basement was roofed over until construction could recommence, and the Halloween

pranks in which wagons were placed on the low roof have entered into local folklore. The "basement church" served from 1909, when it was officially dedicated, until 1913, when, on the eve of another Edmonton financial collapse, Holy Trinity Anglican Church was finally completed.

Strathcona Public Building

Constructed 1913
10505 82nd Avenue
Designated Provincial Historic
Resource February 1985

The Strathcona Public Building (South Edmonton Post Office) exemplifies federal public buildings in Western Canada during the height of pre-war urban development. In 1908 the Strathcona Board of Trade began a campaign to have the federal government provide a public building suitable for a newly proclaimed city. Construction of the post office, which also housed a large customs office, commenced in 1911. The new building opened on Dominion Day 1912, and the clock arrived from England in February 1913, just in time for the implementation of the 1912 amalgamation agreement with Edmonton.

The Strathcona Public Building demonstrates the growing preference for the rational, symmetrical composition of Edwardian Classical Freestyle design and exterior decoration in federal public buildings. Constructed to plans designed by David Ewart, the chief architect of the Canadian Department of Public Works, the building exhibits a departure from the typical Romanesque Revival style frequently used in post offices at the turn of the twentieth century. The original clock tower was "found to be short in height" and was replaced by one ten feet taller in 1914–15.

Faced with red stretcher-bond brick and Tyndall limestone, the building's main façades are symmetrically divided into five bays, with the front corner bays rising into an elegant stone-clad clock tower. Its original four-faced English timepiece, made by J. Smith and Sons Midland Clock Works, Derby, England, and imported by the Strathcona city fathers, remains working in the tower, and pedestrians and motorists on Whyte Avenue still glance up to check the time as they hurry about their daily business. The ornamented limestone entablature, pilasters, contrasting brickwork and shaped voussoirs further identify the old South Edmonton Post Office as an excellent example of federal architecture.

The Strathcona Public Building remains a prominent landmark and reminder of the civic vision of the City of Strathcona, in what is now one of Edmonton's oldest intact historic commercial buildings. The building now accommodates various commercial activities, adding to the vibrancy of Whyte Avenue.

◀ 61A

FOR KING AND EMPIRE
THE GREAT WAR OF 1914-1918

The impossibly immense speculative boom in Western Canada peaked in 1912 with signs of progress seen everywhere in buildings and bridges either completed or under construction.

Rutherford House, home to the first premier, had been completed in Strathcona in 1911. On June 2, 1913, the first train steamed over the newly completed High Level Bridge. The impressive dome of the new Legislature Building rose above the riverbank at the north end of the High Level. On Christmas Day 1914, the first hockey game was played in the new arena. Later named the Gardens, it would host many more memorable landmark games in Edmonton. The McLeod Block became the tallest building in the Canadian west in 1913, while the magnificent Princess Theatre and Hotel Macdonald opened in 1915, their opulence a source of pride for the whole city despite the pall of war.

◀ *The 202nd "Sportsman's" Battalion, Canadian Expeditionary Force, marches on Whyte Avenue past the Strathcona Hotel in February 1916.* 62A

But such signs were the final monuments to the great building boom that had marked the previous quarter century. The first decade of the new City of Edmonton had been marked by tremendous hope and growth. The next would try the spirit and resolve of its people.

Many Edmonton men who had served in the South African War once again rushed to serve king and country when war was declared in Europe in 1914. Many of the city's organizations and influential people were of recent British background or the inheritors of the patriotic traditions still strong in Ontario and the Maritime provinces. The 19th Alberta Dragoons were the first off the mark and the first Edmontonians to see active service in France, departing on February 11, 1915.

The Dragoons were under the command of well-known Edmonton lawyer Col. Frederick C. Jamieson, and another famous local hero, Maj. William A. Griesbach. The Legion of Frontiersmen and the Scottish Pipe Band soon followed.

The 9th Battalion of the Canadian Expeditionary Force was formed largely from the 101st Regiment (Edmonton Fusiliers) under Lt.-Col. E.B. Edwards. The Fusiliers were established in Edmonton in 1908. Later the 51st, 63rd and 66th battalions flocked to the colours. As the need grew for men, the 138th, 194th, 202nd and 218th battalions also were raised in the city.

Edmonton invested its hope and pride in a special unit. Heavy enlistment for the new 49th Battalion of the Canadian Expeditionary Force began on January

▲ *A 1913 aerial view of Edmonton looking north east from McKay Avenue School, showing a substantially built up city centre.* 64A

▲ *The city skyline as it appeared in 1920 was still defined by the dome of the new Provincial Legislature.* 64B

the basketball court in 1915. In 1915 old Fort Edmonton was dismantled, as though to symbolize a dramatic break from the past, and in that same year, prohibition was adopted and the city went officially dry.

4, 1915. This unit was one of very few that retained a connection to its city of origin during the war. In June 1916 the 49th fought at the Battle of Mount Sorrel, and on February 12, 1917 Col. Griesbach, then its commanding officer, was promoted to Brigadier in command of the 1st Canadian Brigade. Lt.-Col. R. H. Palmer succeeded him with the 49th Battalion. The 49th went on to add Vimy Ridge, Hill 70, and Passchendaele to its battle honours. Of the 4,050 men who served in the 49th in France and Belgium, 977 were killed, died of wounds or were missing and presumed dead. Another 2,282 sustained one or more wounds.

With its men away at war, the city struggled to carry on. Women filled a greater role in

civic life, becoming the first in Canada to be eligible to vote in civic and municipal elections. Louise McKinney, later to become a member of the Famous Five, became the first woman elected to a legislature in the British Empire when she served as a member of the Legislative Assembly from 1917 until 1921. Emily Murphy, appointed the first female police magistrate in the British Empire, was immediately challenged in her authority because she failed to meet the definition of a person under the British North America Act. This would lead to the landmark Persons Case decision over a decade later. Other firsts for women included the famous American aviatrix Katherine Stinson flying mail between Calgary and Edmonton, and the Edmonton Commercial Grads taking to

The greatest natural disaster to hit the city occurred on June 28, 1915, when the North Saskatchewan River rose forty-four feet, destroying river valley residential communities and the vital industrial heart of the city with its lumber mills, coal mines, dairies and brickyards. A Canadian Northern Railway train was parked on the Low Level Bridge to add enough weight to keep the bridge from being washed away. Fortunes were lost and it would take years to recover from this blow.

When the men of the celebrated 49th Battalion returned in March 1919, it was to a dramatically changed city. There were more cars on the streets and

▲ *The Great Flood of 1915.* 65A

▲ *Flooding in the river valley community of Rossdale during June 1915.* 65B

▶ *A prohibition parade in 1915.* 65C

more railway connections to the north. Women's styles and attitudes had changed, and movies entertained enthusiastic audiences at palatial movie houses.

Many friends were missing. Just before their return, the city had been devastated by the Spanish influenza pandemic; 450 Edmontonians had died. Many other friends were buried overseas.

Men such as Roland Lines – the architect who had left an indelible imprint on the city before his death in uniform – were numbered among the influential city builders who had been lost.

Others included Alwyn Bramley-Moore, the former MLA who had served as an enlisted man before being killed on the battlefields of France.

In 1919 the Prince of Wales visited the city, and the Edmonton Drill Hall was renamed in his honour shortly thereafter. Private Edgar Hughes, 7th Battalion, willed funds for a War Memorial Fund. Then the city turned back to the task at hand and looked towards the coming decade.

1915 Civic Centre plan by Morrell and Nichols. The timing for this plan was unfortunate as the building boom crashed and financial constraints were intensified by WWI and post-war stagnation. The ability to implement such a grand vision could not longer be sustained. **66A**

▲ 67A

Prince of Wales Armouries

Constructed 1915
10440 108th Avenue
Designated Municipal Historic
Resource August 2004
Designated Provincial Historic
Resource January 1979

The Prince of Wales Armouries, having served the city for close to a century in a number of vital roles, remains a landmark, both architecturally and historically. Originally known as the Edmonton Drill Hall, it was constructed on a seventeen-acre site in 1914–15, at the outbreak of the Great War, to meet the needs of the infantry.

Above the front entrance, the date A.D. 1913 can be seen. This is somewhat misleading, because ground had not even been broken in 1913. A permit for construction valued at $286,000 was issued in May 1914 and the contract with the Department of Public Works is dated July 11, 1914. Lyall & Sons Construction Company Limited of Montreal won the tender to build the Drill Hall. Edmonton's D. E. Ewart and E. C. Hopkins, the supervising architects, were responsible for the impressive design. At the time, Hopkins was described by the *Edmonton Bulletin* as "Edmonton's leading architect," and the "designer of some of the finest buildings in the Dominion of Canada." Hopkins' other designs in Western Canada included the Regina City Hall, the Vancouver Opera House and the Calgary Normal School. Hopkins was Alberta's first provincial architect, appointed in 1905, and went on to design some of the city's most prominent landmarks, including the Great

West Saddlery Company building (1911), the Marshall-Wells Building (1910), the Horne and Pitfield Building (1911), and the Balmoral Block (1913). Hopkins' design for the Edmonton Drill Hall was characteristic of a typical military fortress style that included corner towers and turrets with corbelled parapets and crenellated battlements. Inside the hall can still be seen the massive arched-steel trusses supporting the roof. The floor area tops 65,000 square feet – huge then and huge even now.

Construction was completed in 1915 and both the 51st Battalion and the 233rd Battalion were quartered here. The Drill Hall became better known as the home of the 49th Battalion, Canadian Expeditionary Force, the Edmonton Fusiliers, and The Loyal Edmonton Regiment. You could also find the Garrison Club here.

In 1921 the Drill Hall's name was changed to honour the popular Prince of Wales. The armoury was declared surplus by the Department of National Defence in 1977 and transferred to the Department of Public Works for disposal the following year. But, in a deal among the three levels of government, the federal government got the land for Canada Place, the province got the Federal Public Building, and the City got the armoury site.

Since 1991 the Prince of Wales Armouries has been home to the City of Edmonton Archives, an innovative building-within-a-building design by renowned local architect Fraser Brinsmead. Today it is known as the Prince of Wales Armouries Heritage Centre.

68A ▶

Canada Permanent Building

Constructed 1910
11026–11030 100th Street
Designated Provincial Historic
Resource January 1995

Roland Lines, one of Edmonton's most promising architects, designed the Canada Permanent Building. He would lose his life during the First World War.

The Canada Permanent Building, one of the finest examples of Edwardian Baroque architecture in Edmonton, features Ionic pilasters, an entablatured entrance, an open-topped, segmentally arched pediment, a balustraded parapet and a variety of ornate, classical stone detailing. The building projected solidity, balance and strength, as befitted a conservative financial institution, but it also conveyed its cultural sensitivities through the embellishments. Banks at this time were beginning to bring what they hoped were the refinements of civilization to their major Western Canadian buildings, and the ornate decorations bespoke such aspirations. The company's logo, a winged lighthouse, is carved in stone below a semicircular pediment surmounting the main entrance.

The Canada Permanent Loan Company, the oldest and largest loan institution in Canada at the time, commissioned Roland W. Lines to build an office in downtown Edmonton. Erected in 1910, the building's structural skeleton was constructed of reinforced concrete framing, an innovative construction technique in 1910. When it opened it was described as the city's first fireproof bank.

Canada Permanent Loan Company founder W. Herbert Mason travelled extensively throughout Western Canada to capitalize on the population boom in the Prairies near the turn of the twentieth century. The first Edmonton branch of the company was established in 1901, becoming the company's provincial headquarters.

69A ▲

69B ▶

ROLAND LINES: "HIS INFLUENCE IS STILL EVIDENT TODAY"

Roland Lines was a prominent architect who worked in Edmonton from 1906 to 1915. He was born and raised in England, but was in Alberta in time to apply for membership in the Alberta Association of Architects on February 17, 1906, at its first general meeting. Lines was accepted on the basis of his membership in the Society of Architects of London.

By 1908 he was responsible for several commissions throughout Alberta and Saskatchewan. He designed more than twenty public and private buildings in Edmonton, including the Alexander Taylor School (1906), the Norwood School (1907), and the Collegiate Institute of Strathcona (1907).

A versatile architect, Lines worked in a variety of styles, but much of his work displayed strong classical influences. The Canada Permanent Loan Building (1910) and the Union Bank or North-West Trust Company building (1911) are considered his foremost works. Lines also designed the Royal North-West Mounted Police Barracks and The Villa, the famous home of Col. James Kennedy Cornwall ("Peace River Jim"), still a landmark above Groat Ravine. He also designed the addition to the Jasper House Hotel (now the Hub Hotel).

Lines was chairman of the Alberta Association of Architects in 1912 and became a Fellow of the Royal Institute of British Architects in 1914. He enlisted with the 49th Battalion, Canadian Expeditionary Force, and later transferred to serve with the Royal Engineers. He was killed in France in 1916.

Recently, Lines was honoured posthumously with a lifetime-achievement award from the Edmonton Historical Board. "Though Roland Lines only lived in Edmonton for a few short years, 1906 until 1915," the board noted, "his influence is still evident today."

▲ *Roland Lines* 70A

▲ 71A

▲ 71B

Metals Ltd. Building
Constructed 1914
10186–10190 104th Street
Designated Municipal Historic
Resource December 2002

The Metals Ltd. Building, typical of Warehouse District commercial architecture of the pre-First World War period, has Chicago School of Architecture influences in its robust vertical emphasis enhanced by a strong base and decorative capping. The east façade shows vestiges of the original painted signage on the brick parapet.

The main entrance is located at a chamfered corner on the northeast, facing the street intersection. On either side of the main entrance are two small rose-and-leaf decorations cast in

stone with a cast panel reading "Metals Ltd. Erected 1914" above the door.

The building was designed by noted architects H. A. Magoon and G. H. MacDonald and built by Zenith Construction for Metals Ltd., a wholesale plumbing-and-metal company headquartered in Calgary as Gurney Standard Metal Company Ltd.

Metals Ltd. was incorporated in 1910 as a successor to the earlier company to handle Gurney products. The prominent Calgary board of directors included William Roper Hull, who constructed the Hull Block in 1914. His business interests in Edmonton included a meat-packing plant, operated with Cornelius Gallagher in Gallagher Flats (Cloverdale), and various real estate

interests. Other members included A. E. Cross, Senator James Lougheed and future Prime Minister R. B. Bennett.

Architects H. A. Magoon and G. H. MacDonald were responsible as a partnership or individually for McDougall Methodist Church (1909), Old St. Stephen's College (1910–11), the Tegler Building (1911), the Rothesay Apartments (1914), the H. V. Shaw Block (1914), the Public Library Building (1923), Robertson-Wesley Church (1914) and the Federal Building (1954), to name a few.

In 2003, Worthington Properties with admirable sensitivity restored the Metals Building to its earlier glory with the help of a grant from the City to spearhead the reclamation of 104th Street.

Princess Theatre

Constructed 1915
10335–10337 82nd Avenue
Designated Provincial Historic
Resource May 1995

Edmonton entrepreneur and cinema pioneer John Wellington McKernan opened the Princess Theatre as a grand 660-seat vaudeville and movie house on Whyte Avenue in 1915 in the midst of the economic collapse during the First World War. Times were hard, but after almost ten months of financial struggle, the theatre's doors opened on March 8 to considerable public acclaim.

The opening ceremony featured a benefit concert for the recently organized chapter of the Imperial Order of the Daughters of the Empire, associated with the 19th Alberta Dragoons, B Squadron, which was still stationed at the fairly new Connaught Armoury. The event was billed as "one of the most enjoyable events of the season and of a decided patriotic nature."

McKernan purchased the site from Strathcona businessmen Robert Ritchie in March 1913 and contracted the prominent Strathcona architectural firm of Wilson and Herrald, designers of many of the impressive public buildings in Strathcona during the construction boom of the preceding five

◀ 72A

years. What McKernan had in mind was a "palace theatre" that he hoped would stand proudly among its new neighbours. The ultimate design of the new theatre appeared to be inspired by the Empire Theatre in downtown Edmonton, which had a colonial façade. With the exception of the British Columbia marble used for the façade, which distinguished the Princess as the only marble-fronted structure west of Winnipeg, all materials and labour were supplied from Edmonton. The vestibule and lobby were finished in marble and tile, stained glass crowned the double entrance doors, and a grand staircase led directly to the balcony.

The stage, on which vaudeville and musical programs were performed, was the largest in a cinema in Western Canada. The first regular program to play at the Princess was headlined by the Mary Pickford feature The Eagle's Mate, which played March 10–11, and which became one of the most successful films released by the newly formed Famous Players group. According to the publicity of the day, it provided a "thrilling picture of life and romance in the West Virginia Mountains."

John Wellington McKernan's family was originally from Ontario. The first McKernan to come west was Constable James McKernan, who enlisted in the North West Mounted Police in 1873 and rode west on the Great Trek of 1874. His brother

▲   73A

Robert joined him in November 1878, and they later settled in what would become the southwestern district of Strathcona, where James began farming near the lake that would later bear his name. The first child born in the west to Robert and his wife Sara in October 1880, was John Wellington McKernan, who would become one of Strathcona's principal pioneers and builders. During the pre-war real estate boom, he amassed a fortune and, to further improve his prospects, he seized the novel opportunity presented by motion pictures.

Four years before John McKernan entered the theatre business, the Empire Theatre was built in downtown Edmonton, becoming

the first theatre to feature motion pictures rather than vaudeville acts. Within a year of its construction, it was renamed the Bijou. Within six years the Bijou was joined in the downtown by the Grand and Orpheum theatres. In 1910 John McKernan established the Gem Theatre in Strathcona, the first movie theatre south of the river, and later the south side Bijou and Princess theatres. In 1913 the bottom fell out of Edmonton and Strathcona's frantic real estate markets. Fortunes had been made and lost, but in 1913 entrepreneurs mostly lost. The excitement and optimism that had animated the twin cities of Edmonton and Strathcona since their amalgamation in 1912 was swept away and would not

return for many years. Of course, the McKernans were not immune from this economic malaise, although they weathered the storm better than many. Nevertheless, John McKernan was forced to close the Gem and the Bijou, and after that he pinned his hopes solely on the Princess.

On September 23, 1915, McKernan received a bulletin from Famous Players explaining that "On account of the boat Hesperian having been torpedoed by a German submarine, it will be necessary to skip two 'Weeklies'," a photo news service that had become a popular part of the Princess's repertoire in April 1915.

On February 18, 1919, John Wellington McKernan died during the great influenza pandemic that swept the world following the war, claiming more casualties than the war itself. The flu hit Edmonton on October 19, 1918, when the first forty-one cases were reported. To handle the prospect of hundreds of stricken citizens, Dr. Heber C. Jamieson, acting director of bacteriology, set up flu wards in schools, armouries and the top floor of the Macdonald Hotel – in fact, anywhere space could be obtained.

By February 1919, the worst was over, but in mid-month John McKernan contracted the virus and quickly succumbed, still a young man. With his death the first chapter of the Princess Theatre's history came to an end.

While the theatre would remain in the McKernan family until 1958, by 1919 it was leased and managed by Alexander Entwistle, who would own the major theatre chain in Edmonton from the 1920s through the 1940s.

In 1976 the Old Strathcona Foundation rescued the aging Princess from demolition. The rundown building was lovingly restored, and its doors were reopened in 1978. The reopening signalled a new atmosphere of rejuvenation as historical Strathcona was undergoing a rebirth under the aegis of the Old Strathcona Foundation. The Princess is now a repertory theatre, having added in 1999 a second screen, Princess II, in the basement with a 100-seat capacity.

◀ 74A

▲ 75A

▲ 75B

Hotel Grand (Hagmann Block)

Constructed 1913
10765 98th Street
Designated Municipal Historic
Resource January 2006

The Hotel Grand, also known as the Hagmann Block, is a four-storey commercial block displaying two primary façades. Located in the McCauley neighbourhood, it is a fine example of the commercial architecture of its day, displaying the popular Classical Revival influence in its tan brick, outsized ground-floor storefronts, pressed metal cornices above the ground floor and at the roofline, and precast neoclassical details.

The Hotel Grand was an early mixed-use hotel that accommodated the area's seasonal and travelling population during the time of Edmonton's rapid development as a commercial centre in the early twentieth century. John Hagmann built the Grand at the end of Edmonton's pre-war real estate boom as an investment property. At the time he farmed land on what is now the Hagmann Estate in northwest Edmonton. This farm in 1927 would provide the land for Edmonton's first "air harbour." That same year the hotel was converted to the Convent of the Assumption.

The Hagmann Block also indicates the development of McCauley, one of Edmonton's oldest neighbourhoods, named for Matthew McCauley. He was Edmonton's first mayor, a member of the provincial parliament, and chairman of Edmonton's first school board. The McCauley area emerged as a financial and business district with hotels clustered to the south, a red-light district to the northeast and a residential area to the north.

McLeod Block

Constructed 1913–1915
10132–10136 100th Street
Designated Municipal Historic
Resource May 2001
Designated Provincial Historic
Resource January 1995

The McLeod Block is a nine-storey, brick-and-terra-cotta structure designed in the Chicago Commercial style on a prominent corner in downtown Edmonton. The building expresses the refined neoclassicism reinvented at the Chicago World's Fair of 1893 that virtually came to dominate American cities in the early part of the twentieth century.

The McLeod Block was patterned after the Polson Block in Spokane, Washington, and was designed by the same architect, J. K. Dow. The Edmonton building features numerous Edwardian-era embellishments and is the only remaining terra-cotta-clad building in the city. Finished in a luxurious style that added prestige to the address, it featured Italian Pavanosse marble in the entrance and corridor wainscoting. When it opened, the McLeod Block boasted the status of being the tallest building between Winnipeg and the West Coast.

The McLeod Block was developed by Kenneth McLeod, who arrived from Ontario in 1891. He remained the sole owner until 1929. He wanted to build a structure that was even taller than the Tegler Building (1911–83), and he achieved his goal, holding the local record for height until the Macdonald Annex was built in 1951. As a result of the war and postwar financial doldrums, the McLeod Block would not be fully occupied until 1924.

The McLeod Block's proximity to the former downtown post office, land titles office, courthouse and city hall attracted doctors, lawyers, insurance and grain agents, and many other prominent tenants. The Hon. A. C. Rutherford, the first premier of Alberta, conducted his law business from the McLeod. The building's prominence remained until the 1960s when new modern office buildings attracted the city's elite clientele.

▲ 76A

H. V. Shaw Block

Constructed 1914
10229 105th Street
Designated Municipal Historic
Resource November 2001

A cigar factory was originally located on the main floor of the H. V. Shaw Block and later moved to the top floor as the building was completed. During the first weeks of the First World War, shortly after completion of the building, Shaw lent one floor to Lt.-Col. William Griesbach of the 49th Battalion, Canadian Expeditionary Force, for squad drills during the mobilization of forces. Many buildings in Edmonton were pressed into use in support of the war effort.

The H. V. Shaw Block is a factory and warehouse characterized by Chicago School of Architecture and Gothic elements. The style was rare in Edmonton, especially for a warehouse.

The building was designed to be fireproof through the use of a reinforced, cast-in-place concrete structural system that was innovative for the time. The western façade, one of the most decorative among Edmonton's early warehouses, is broken into three sections, common in the Chicago style, with a solid, defined classical base, a vertical emphasis through the use of piers, repetitive, recessed spandrels and a decorative capping at the parapet level. The piers, clad in

77A ▶

Tyndall stone and red tapestry brick have a Gothic buttress feel. The recessed main entrance is bordered with arched voussoirs and evenly spaced, cast-stone patterning. Stylized cast-stone leaf designs are also set into the brick wall on either side of the main entrance, reminiscent of those on the Metals Ltd. Building, also designed by the same architectural firm of Magoon and MacDonald. Railway access was available from the rear of the building. Various tenants have used the south building façade for painted-sign advertising over the years.

Harry V. Shaw arrived in Edmonton from Minneapolis in 1901. As a teenager in St. Paul, he had been trained in cigar-making, and in Edmonton, with two assistants, Shaw founded a cigar-manufacturing factory

in the Humberstone Block. The cigars were hand-rolled, using raw materials imported from Havana and Sumatra, and the company came to be known for its Palma, Major Reno and La Consequentia cigars. In 1906 Shaw expanded to the downtown Masonic Building. Output grew to over a million cigars by 1908, and in 1914 Shaw constructed a building to house his expanding operation, which three years later had grown to ninety employees, making him manager of one of the largest crews of skilled labour in the city. Shaw had purchased the property on 105th Street and 102nd Avenue in 1905 in anticipation of business growth. The architectural firm of Magoon and MacDonald was commissioned by Shaw for his project. They also designed Shaw's residence

(built in 1913, demolished in 1978).

In 1919, after suffering severe economic setbacks, Shaw was forced to close his factory. He subsequently lost the building to his creditors, along with his mansion on Victoria Avenue, which went to the city for unpaid taxes. Shaw had apparently overextended himself with the simultaneous construction of his business block and mansion. The failure of the factory was also due to the rise in popularity of cigarettes during the war and the closing of saloons during prohibition. He tried to start another cigar factory on Stony Plain Road at 124th Street, but this too failed. Shaw died in Edmonton in 1959.

Hecla Block

Constructed 1914
10141 95th Street
Designated Municipal Historic
Resource November 1999

The Hecla Block once represented a comfortably adequate apartment building, its red low-fired brick exterior suggesting welcoming warmth. Buff stone trim contrasts with the textured brick in the arches over the windows, at the corners as quoins, in string courses above the second and third storeys, and in diamond-shaped panels between the second-floor windows. The two main faces present a classical cornice that some describe as Edwardian Classicism.

The plan had to be skewed to accommodate the oblique angle between 101st Avenue and 95th Street, resulting in a building shaped somewhat like a slanted letter J with many rooms being trapezoidal in shape. Such adaptive designs, calculated to accommodate oddly shaped lots, were relatively common in a time when real estate costs were usually high.

Apparently named after Mount Hecla, the largest and most well-known volcano in Iceland, the apartment block was built by Icelandic-Canadian John Johnson, who arrived in Canada with his family in 1876 to settle in Gimli, Manitoba, Canada's largest Icelandic community and a part

▲ 79A

of what was then the Republic of New Iceland. Hecla Island and Hecla Village are a short distance north of Gimli. From there Johnson moved to Markerville, Alberta, another predominantly Icelandic community, and the home of the Icelandic national poet Stephan G. Stephansson. Johnson relocated to Edmonton in 1902, where he established himself as a builder, constructing some sixty-five houses and two apartment buildings in the east-central part of the city. The Riverview Apartments, his other block, still stands across 95th Street from the Hecla. In the past twenty years, both buildings were ravaged by fire and fully restored to residential use.

Johnson retained the local firm of Hardie and Martland, "building designers and structural engineers," to design his apartment building. Prior to the Hecla Apartments, Hardie had designed the J. C. McDougall Residence (1912) on 103rd Street, the Tyrone Apartments on 99th Avenue and the Armstrong Block (1912) on 104th Street. John Martland would become the municipal architect for the City of Edmonton in 1919, a position he held for eighteen years. The partners also designed the Sacred Heart Church (1913) on 96th Street and 108th Avenue.

In 1924 the bank foreclosed, and Johnson lost control of the Hecla Block, nothing out of the ordinary in the early days of rampant real estate speculation that characterized one of the city's first booms.

A DECADE OF HOPE AND PERSISTENCE
1919-1929

The Roaring Twenties did not roar quite so loudly in Edmonton as in many other places. It seemed more a time to find new direction for the city as it gradually recovered from the devastation of war and the influenza pandemic.

The discovery of oil at Fort Norman in 1920 resulted in a brief outburst of oil speculation, but it soon fizzled. Perhaps the only bright spot was the city's role as an agricultural supply centre for the growing agricultural industry in central and northern Alberta, partly stimulated through the efforts of the Soldiers Settlement Board. In this atmosphere, people hungered for opportunities to help each other and seek strength for the future.

On January 24, 1921, the Edmonton Federation of Community Leagues was established as one response to the deep need for a sense of

◄ *A view of downtown Edmonton in 1928, looking southeast across the Post Office, Hotel Macdonald and McLeod Building towards the river valley.* 80A

fellowship. It rapidly grew to the largest organization of its kind in Canada, with both social and political power.

Hopes for postwar reconstruction and civil re-establishment were dampened by many factors, but chief among them was the high unemployment rate among returning military personnel. Though groups such as the Great War Veterans Association – which built Memorial Hall as a gathering place – championed the cause of veterans, many of the disenchanted found little opportunity and joined the brief and partial general strike that hit the city between May 26 and 31, 1919. The Winnipeg General Strike overshadowed the local strike, but the sense of bitterness among veterans ran deep. The militant One Big Union, established in Calgary that same year, soon had adherents across the West.

Though life in Edmonton during the 1920s did not rival the excitement of the pre-war era, it was not without its diversions and excitements. At the beginning of the war, Principal J. Percy Page (later to become Lieutenant-Governor of Alberta) had started teaching physical education to young women at McDougall Commercial High School. Little did he or the world know where this would lead. When Dr. James Naismith, the inventor of basketball, watched the Grads play in 1925, he pronounced them "the finest basketball team that ever stepped on a floor." After the war the Grads rose to world prominence, and Edmontonians took special pride in their achievements. At the 1924 Paris Olympic Games, the Grads won all matches to become world champions but did not take home gold medals because women's basketball was not recognized as an official event until many years later. They

would eventually hold 108 titles at all levels of competition including another three Olympic titles. When the team disbanded in 1940, they were credited with an astonishing 96 per cent of 522 games, a record unrivalled by any North American basketball team.

New technologies helped ease the bleak winters, especially after the first radio station went on air on May 1, 1922. CJCA first broadcast from a corner of the newsroom in the *Edmonton Journal*, where the communications pioneer G. R. A. Rice began his career. In 1927 the University of Alberta launched radio station CKUA, today a unique listener-supported provincial network. Young and old gathered to skate at McKernan Lake or at the new Central

Skating Rink that opened in 1922 on Jasper Avenue and 112th Street. The Edmonton Newsboys Band, first organized in 1914 by the *Edmonton Journal*, really came into its own during the 1920s when it was acclaimed as one of the finest bands in the world. Others in the arts community made efforts to find a voice again after the war, and in 1923 the Art and Historical Museum Association was organized under Mrs. David Bowman, Dr. R. B. Wells and William Johnstone. Prohibition was repealed in 1923, and the Alberta Liquor Control Board took control of alcohol distribution and sales. Control was the watchword, and beer parlours were required to have separate entrances for men and for "Ladies and Escorts."

Until the 1920s the city had many coal mines within its limits. On November 9, 1923, Mayor D. M. Duggan lit a flare from the first natural gas to arrive via the pipeline from the Viking gas field located east of the city. Natural gas began to replace coal for heating homes, and the familiar coal delivery wagons disappeared over the next three decades.

The new Canadian National Railway station opened to much fanfare and huge crowds on St. Patrick's Day 1928. Few buildings had risen during the 1920s, especially when compared with the boom preceding the war. For many, this event heralded what they hoped would be a more prosperous future.

Emily Murphy Residence
Constructed circa 1912
11011 88th Avenue
Designated Provincial Historic
Resource June 1977 and June 2000

Women fought for and won the right to vote in Alberta during the First World War. The war gave women such as Emily Murphy the opportunity to exercise their voice in the public political debate of suffrage, prohibition and other issues.

The Emily Murphy Residence is something of a cultural shrine located on University of Alberta land in the historic Garneau district. Her simple home features clapboard siding on the first storey, a shingled façade on the second, and a clipped gable roof. It was constructed around 1912 from materials and a design fairly typical of the time. It features several Craftsman style embellishments, including eave brackets and exposed rafters on the exterior, and panelled doors, square staircase balustrades and newel posts on the interior.

Emily Murphy was a renowned jurist, social activist, and author who lived in this house from 1919 until her death in 1933. Born in Cookstown, Ontario, in 1868, Murphy came west with her husband in 1887. She arrived in Edmonton in 1907 and quickly established herself as an outspoken advocate for the rights of women and children. Passage of the Dower Act in 1911 is

▲ 83A

credited to her influence. She was appointed a magistrate in 1916, the first woman in the British Empire to attain this position.

In 1927, at a meeting in her home, Murphy initiated the work of Alberta's "Famous Five" – including Nellie McClung, Henrietta Muir Edwards, Louise McKinney and Irene Parlby – in their effort to have women recognized as persons eligible to hold Canadian Senate positions under the provisions of the British North America Act. The British Privy Council decided in favour of the group's petition in 1929, a landmark still celebrated today. Murphy also held posts as president of the Federated Women's Institutes of Canada (1919–21), vice-president of the National Council of Women (1918–26), director of the Canadian Council of Child Welfare (1923–27) and president of the Canadian Women's Press Club (1913–20), among others. She was better known as Janey Canuck following the publication of her first novel Janey Canuck Abroad, and her Western Canadian stories still remain popular. Her writing on issues such as immigration, narcotics and health also were influential, although more recently her views on eugenics have aroused heated debate.

The Emily Murphy Residence later served as University of Alberta student housing and now, appropriately, is home to the University of Alberta's Student Legal Services.

▲ 84A

Bentley Farmhouse

Constructed circa 1920
20450 34th Street
Designated Municipal Historic
Resource November 1999

The brick Bentley farmhouse located in the northeast part of Edmonton is a rare example of a period farm surviving within the boundaries of Edmonton. The city was located at the hub of an active agricultural community in earlier times, but as urban growth consumed the surrounding farmlands, farm buildings frequently disappeared during subdivision and subsequent development. Some remain within residential districts, anonymously and anomalously hunkered down among their more recent neighbours.

The Bentley farm, however, remains in a farm setting, reminding us of a time when the city was largely devoted to supplying the men and women who worked the land.

▲ 85A

Trudel House
Constructed 1929
8134 Jasper Avenue
Designated Municipal Historic
Resource June 2000

Architect Richard Palin Blakey designed
this clinker-brick Craftsman bungalow on
a Jasper Avenue lot with an impressive view
of the North Saskatchewan River valley. The
first owner, Ludger (Louis) Joseph Trudel,
president of Trudel Fur Manufacturers, had
purportedly profited through a contract to
sell buffalo coats to the police, a common
measure against the bitter Alberta winters
until the disappearance of the buffalo. The
contractor was A. O. Josey, who also built
the Bank of Commerce, Birks Building and
the Provincial Administration Building.

Ad Josey lived to age 101, becoming
for a time Edmonton's oldest citizen.

Ernest Brown Block (Brighton Block)
Constructed 1911–12
9670 Jasper Avenue
Designated Municipal Historic
Resource July 2001

The Ernest Brown Block has been described as a "classicized version of the Edwardian Commercial style." Twelve bays wide, its walls of red brick are relieved by trim of buff stone. Emphasis on the central and end bays is characteristic of designs influenced by the Beaux Arts classicism of the era. The same trend is seen in a grander scale in the McLeod Building, the Legislature Building and the Bowker Building, and in smaller scale in the W.W. Arcade Building and Lodge Hotel located on the same block.

The Ernest Brown Block was constructed in two stages in 1911–12. The two portions of the building were identical, with the eastern part completed first. The parapet and cornice of the first part were altered at the time the second portion was completed in 1912. Brown placed his name on the building in the central pediment that reads Ernest Brown Block 1912, and he added Everything Photographic to the parapet wall to advertise his photography studio and supply store. James Henderson (1861–1932), one of Edmonton's leading architects, designed the Ernest Brown

◀ 86A

Block. Henderson was originally from England, but moved to Edmonton some time before 1907. He designed many private residences, including the Glenora mansion of Attorney-General Charles Cross (1912, demolished in 1977) and several civic and commercial buildings, such as the Moser and Ryder Block (1910, refaced in 1944), the First Street Fire Hall (1910) and the Children's Shelter (1911–12). In 1907 he was elected a fellow of the Royal Institute of British Architects and joined the Alberta Association of Architects, becoming president in 1914.

Peter Rule Construction Company was contracted to erect the building. Peter

Rule later became an architect for Alberta Government Telephones, but he is better known as the father of Peter Rule, Jr., and John Rule, principals in the prolific and influential architectural firm Rule Wynn Rule. Soon after the eastern part of the building was completed, the Peter Rule construction firm established its offices on the second floor.

In addition to serving as Brown's studio and photographic supply establishment, the ground floor housed other businesses, including Harry Taylor, a men's clothier, and a printing and stationery store. Brown's enlargement department and his picture-framing plant were located in the

basement. The upper floors were leased as offices and apartments. According to the Edmonton Journal in 1913, the apartments were available "in suites of from one to four rooms with bath, and the building embodies every modern feature, including fireproof interior, fire escape and conveniences for refined home life, containing eighty rooms, besides its business department." The article also described the studio and reception salon as "the most complete and well appointed, not to say beautiful … in the West." The marble walls, Italian terrazzo floor and tropical palms added to the refined atmosphere of Brown's Studio.

Apart from his photographic career, Brown was a community activist concerned about the city and its less fortunate inhabitants. In 1906 he organized Edmonton's first "tag day," a day of special events, to raise money for the Royal Alexandra Hospital. Brown also once led a hunger march for the unemployed.

Brown continued to operate his business in the building until he suffered financial difficulties in the early 1920s. He continued to own the property until 1923, but when Credit Foncier Franco-Canadian received the title in 1924, it ceased to be known as the Brown Block. Brown moved to Vegreville, east of Edmonton, where he opened a small studio and devoted himself to photography, cataloguing his collection, and writing a history, The Birth of the West. He received various commissions from firms, including the Hudson's Bay Company and the Canadian Pacific Railway, which required photographs of the west.

In 1929 Brown returned to Edmonton to realize his dream of establishing a museum dedicated to the history of the West. He began the project with a photographic exhibit, and in 1933 he established the Brown Museum (also called the Pioneer Days Museum) in Haddon Hall on 97th Street. In 1947 the Province of Alberta purchased his collection. Today the Ernest Brown collection is one of the most important photographic holdings in the Provincial Archives, and is well represented in this book.

The Brighton Block has housed a variety of businesses and offices. It was the location of the Georgia Steam Baths between 1946 and 2002. The basement was occupied by the city's first cafeteria, the American Dairy Lunch, owned by George Spillios and Harry Lingas. The west storefront was modified around 1950, while the east storefront retains its original windows,

transoms and reveals. Today the building has been restored to its former name and once again is known as the Brown Block.

ERNEST BROWN

Ernest Brown was born in Middlesbrough, England, in 1877 and immigrated to Canada in 1903. He arrived in Edmonton that year to work with C. W. Mathers, a well-known Edmonton photographer. Brown began his career as an assistant in Mathers' Jasper Avenue studio, which was Edmonton's oldest photographic studio, having been established in 1885 as a branch of the Calgary firm of William Hanson Boorne and Ernest G. May. The Mathers gallery was located in a small frame building with a gable roof that housed an art gallery as well as the photographic studio. The success of Mathers' firm led to an expansion of the building a decade later, and by 1904 there was a new building with a false front. Three years later, plate-glass windows were installed, reputedly the first in Edmonton.

Ernest Brown acquired Mathers' business, building and photographic collection in 1904. A few years later, he began making plans for the construction of the large office and studio building that stands today. Brown's business flourished with the ever-increasing demand for portrait photography in the young city. His new building was designed to accommodate a studio, workshop and offices for his expanding business. The pre-war boom years proved lucrative for Brown. His massive photographic collection was used for one of Edmonton's first museums and today is an important collection in the Provincial Archives of Alberta.

◀   89A

McTaggart-Haight Residence

Constructed circa 1922
11530 95A Street
Designated Municipal Historic
Resource November 2004

This Craftsman bungalow is a common example of a 1920s middle-income single-family dwelling. An enclosed porch with an exposed gable characterizes the front elevation. The porch is framed by timber columns, with eight large fixed windows with smaller rectangular panes running above them. The gable end has shingle siding with a band of curved patterned shingles in the middle and exposed eaves with three decorative supporting brackets. This neat little cottage was probably built to a catalogue design with construction in part undertaken by the original owner, John Lawson Haight.

▲ 90A

Haight was born in Oak River, Manitoba, in 1891, attended normal school in Calgary, and by 1913 was teaching in rural schools in southern Alberta. In 1916 he joined the Royal Flying Corps and spent two years as a prisoner of war. In 1919 Haight began teaching at Parkdale School. In September 1921 he was transferred to H. Allen Gray, and around 1922 he built his house. In 1925, complaining that the stress of teaching was "sapping" his health, Haight sold the house and moved his family to the warmer climate of St. Petersburg, Florida.

The McTaggart family bought the house in 1925. John Wesley McTaggart was born in 1894 in Alvinston, Ontario, and attended school in St. Thomas. He moved to Edmonton in 1924 and began working as an accountant, later serving as manager of MacCosham Storage for twenty-five years.

▲ *By the 1902s Jasper Avenue's commercial frontages became more established and architecturally imposing, rapidly replacing the original timber structures and boom town buildings.*
91A

ENDURANCE AND DETERMINATION
THE GREAT DEPRESSION OF 1929-1939

The first neon signs lit Jasper Avenue in 1929, but their glow turned out to be more ominous than merry as the shock waves of the Wall Street crash on Black Thursday, October 24, 1929, reached Edmonton and the Canadian West slipped into another decade of economic stagnation.

During the infamous Dirty Thirties, so-called "porridge kitchens" came to symbolize the plight of the unemployed. Those desperate men lucky enough to secure government "relief work" on city streets were provided with barely enough to feed their families. An underground economy grew up in the shantytown on the Grierson Hill dump, where men sold recycled items to Edmontonians who were barely better off than they were. On December 20, 1932, hundreds of distressed people converged on Market Square in the city centre to protest their plight. With little warning, they were dispersed by Mounties on horses charging into the crowd, cracking heads with clubs.

Throughout the Great Depression, the Prairies witnessed the rise of a radical,

◀ *A welcome gate awaits the Royal Tour at the Alberta Legislature on June 2, 1939.* 92A

exciting spectrum of new political philosophies such as the Co-operative Commonwealth Federation and the Social Credit movement. The Communist Party voice became more strident and grew in popular appeal. Everywhere, people were seeking a solution to their distress, and religious movements became ever more popular among the hopeless.

In these desperate times, the arts suffered. The Edmonton Symphony Orchestra was forced to disband in 1932. Nevertheless, believers in the importance of the arts persisted, among them Elizabeth Sterling, who became the first woman to serve as a provincial drama director in 1937. With Donald Cameron, Sterling helped establish the Banff School of Fine Arts, as well as numerous local drama groups. Shining lights such as Sterling kept the arts alive during the dark years.

City businesses and industries were unable to sustain much building during the 1930s. Many buildings were modified and converted into other uses as firms faltered or failed.

Building in the public sector was an exception. Edmonton had a long history of developing public utilities such as the Rossdale site, which had been used for power generation since 1902. Beginning in 1931, Edmonton Power built the first part of the existing complex that now includes the Low Pressure Plant, Pump House No. 1, and the Administration Building.

This period also witnessed a change in some of the architecture being designed and built. Amongst some of the more "traditional" domestic properties being constructed, more modern structures began to emerge, with simpler lines and less detailing. The

◀ *Clarke Stadium named after Mayor Joe Clarke who fought hard to get this landmark built.* 94A

for years and would be the site of many triumphs in the City of Champions.

By the late 1930s, newspapers began carrying ominous stories of the rising tide of violence in Europe and Asia and warned of the coming war. On June 2, 1939, King George VI and Queen Elizabeth visited Edmonton, and thousands of men, women and schoolchildren crowded bleachers along Kingsway Avenue, renamed in honour of the Royal visit. The Canadian Royal Tour was seen as an omen of the impending war that would call on many young people waving a sea of Union Jacks to make the greatest sacrifice for their country.

modern era had begun. In Edmonton, Art Deco never really caught on, but a more muted style called Moderne captured some of the Art Deco characteristics of flat horizontal lines, with occasional details around key features such as doors.

The Depression years marked the true heyday of Mayor "Fighting Joe" Clarke, who served five terms as mayor and eight as city councillor between 1912 and 1937. Clarke moved to Edmonton in 1908 to practise law and would run twenty-six times for city council, running for mayor sixteen times. During his second term as

alderman, he sided with Mayor William McNamara in his bid to stifle reformers who wanted to run prostitution and gambling out of town. This alliance ended when the two came to blows in a council meeting, earning him the sobriquet "Fighting Joe."

His flamboyant style was a needed antidote to the times. It was Clarke who used his relationship with Prime Minister Mackenzie King to secure a lease on the federal land near the old Edmonton penitentiary to build a sports stadium to provide desperately needed employment. Clarke Stadium remained a landmark

Like the Great War of 1914–18, the coming war would transform the city. Aviation pioneers Wop May, Vic Horner and Punch Dickins would return to train another generation of young airmen, and soon the massive mobilization would be underway.

Immigration Hall

Constructed 1930
10534 100th Street
Designated Municipal Historic
Resource September 2009

Immigration Hall is one of only three surviving post-First World War immigration halls in Western Canada and is a significant representation of that era of the province's history. Additionally, it is an excellent example of the influence of the federal Department of Public Works, reflecting the work of its architect, Thomas William Fuller.

Immigration Hall, characterized by its classically proportioned symmetrical façade and flat roof, is situated in a prominent corner location at 100th Street and 105A Avenue, and is separated from Edmonton's downtown core by the former Canadian National Railway yard in the McCauley neighbourhood. It makes use of superior building materials including Flemish-bond, variegated-colour combed brick, smooth-faced Tyndall stone and granite steps. It is further distinguished by a continuous sheet-metal projecting cornice with a simple brick parapet above and a double-height central entrance detailed in Tyndall stone,

with a shallow projecting cornice above the entrance doors and a blank panel above, capped with an arched window surround with keystone. There is a segmental, arched Chicago window above the central entry and regular banks of double-assembly windows, with those on the upper floors set between broad, shallow brick pilasters, and those in the basement inserted into the Tyndall-stone base. Although understated in many ways, Immigration Hall is a stylish expression of its type.

Designed in 1927 and constructed in 1930, it is the last and most elaborate of

a series of functionally similar buildings built across the Prairie provinces over a 50-year period. It symbolizes the federal government's immigration policy, which encouraged western settlement as part of the National Policy from the beginning of Canadian presence in the Northwest and remains a significant part of western Canadian history to the present.

Immigration Halls were an important component of this policy, as they provided free short-term accommodation for agricultural settlers. This building was constructed as a result of an ambitious federal immigration policy, but was only nominally utilized due to the onset of the Depression and a reversal in 1930 of the previous "open-door" policy. The location of Immigration Hall north of the downtown core and the former CNR railway yard illustrates how these facilities were strategically constructed near main railway stations to accommodate the influx of new immigrants. Although the building ceased operations as an Immigration Hall in 1951, it maintained a similar function as offices of the Department of Citizenship and Immigration, and as a citizenship court until 1969.

Furthermore, Immigration Hall is a good example of the conservative architectural expression of the federal government during this time period. Traditional architectural styles remained popular during the interwar period and this design demonstrates the late persistence of the Classical Revival style that had been introduced at the turn of the nineteenth century. Here, classicism has been stripped to its essentials, with strictly ordered symmetry, minimal ornamentation and superior cladding materials providing dignity to an otherwise utilitarian structure.

Immigration Hall has additional heritage value for its association with Thomas William Fuller (1865-1951), chief architect of the Federal Department of Public Works. Fuller, the son of previous Chief Architect Thomas Fuller, had a life-long career with the DPW, and assumed the role of chief architect from 1918 to 1936. He was responsible for the design of many military buildings and armouries across the country, as Canada prepared for the First World War. Throughout the 1920s and 1930s, the DPW remained conservative in its design approach, as demonstrated in this building by the late persistence of the influence of the Classical Revival styles. The 1954 addition was also designed by the office of the chief architect's branch of the federal Department of Public Works. Meant to match the original structure, the 1954 addition used similar materials and detailing.

◀ 96A

Oblats Maison Provinciale

Constructed 1935
9916 110th Street
Designated Municipal Historic
Resource August 2004
Designated Provincial Historic
Resource October 2001

This impressive building is a reminder of the significant role played in Alberta history by Oblate missionaries such as Father Lacombe, who built the missions at Lac Ste-Anne, Saint Albert and Midnapore.

This rare Federal style building, deceptively simple in appearance is surprisingly expressive in its detailing. The front, east-facing façade displays its original brickwork with a Flemish bonded-brick pattern and quoin detailing at the edges. A central raised door and pediment, with arched entrance and circular fanlight surmounting the timber doors, adds to the impressive statement. Brick voussoirs and the keystone in the door arch complete the effect, as does a prominent metal cornice with modillions. The octagonal cupola and metal cross are distinguishing features.

97A ▶

Balfour Manor

Constructed 1912, Renovated 1939
10139 116th Street
Designated Municipal Historic
Resource July 2005

The Balfour Manor is an excellent example of a building that has evolved over time through adaptive reuse. Its architectural merit lies in its current architectural form, and its significance is enhanced by its earlier history.

This asymmetrical building was designed originally as Fire Hall No. 4 for the west end, which then consisted of Oliver, Glenora, Westmount and Inglewood. Around 1911 the Edmonton Fire Department acquired the land and erected a new hall to serve this growing new part of town, and it opened on February 13, 1912. The hall was built to accommodate horses and horse-drawn equipment, but as more modern machinery became more prevalent, the last horses were finally sold in 1921 and the hall closed "due to motorization of the department."

Beginning in 1922, the building's main floor was used as a garage by Jarvis Hutchinson and then by Harry Whitehead. In 1933 Midland Rapid Transit Bus Company took over the building and remained there until 1939. While the building's ground floor functioned as a garage, the upper floor was residential, usually with the proprietors residing in the units.

▲ 98A

The original brick building was extensively remodelled and modernized in 1939 into an eclectic state-of-the-art apartment building with Mission and Art Deco influences. The Balfour remains one of only a few remaining examples of the Art Moderne style built to this modest scale. An additional floor increased its height and two storeys were added at the rear to provide a total of ten suites. Fluted stucco columns, horizontal bandings and a decorative stepped and curved parapet were added, and by the time the building was finished in smooth stucco it bore no resemblance to its original look or use. Edmonton contractor Joseph N. Cote completed the rebuilding and restyling of the old fire hall.

Chandler Barn

Constructed 1912,
10828 125th Street
Designated Municipal Historic
Resource December 2008

Changes made to the Chandler Barn, during the 1920s or 1930s, tell an important part of the building history and the broader history of Edmonton. The barn, located at the rear of a lot mid-block within the Westmount Architectural Heritage Area, is significant for its association with the first residential development of the Westmount neighbourhood and as a reminder of the increasing presence and importance of the automobile in Edmonton.

This barn, and later garage, characterized by a gambrel roof and shiplap siding, was built in 1912 and is significant as part of the early development in Westmount, one of Edmonton's oldest prestige neighbourhoods. Malcolm Groat, who settled in the area in 1878, opened the land to development in the years preceding the First World War. Many of the newly successful entrepreneurial and professional class were attracted to Westmount by its proximity to downtown and the promise of streetcar connection between downtown and the west end. Edgar W. Chandler, lumber inspector for the Dominion government, was among these young professionals; he purchased his lot in 1912, building a home at the front and a barn at the rear.

▲ 99A

This building represents an important transition in modes of transportation and lifestyles in Edmonton. It was constructed with a single door on the west elevation to admit a carriage, while a hayloft in the half-storey above was used to store feed for a horse, also kept in the barn. Although J. H. Morris brought the first automobile to Edmonton in 1904, cars remained relatively uncommon in 1912 and were used mostly for "auto touring," with the horse-and-carriage being a common form of urban transportation until the First

World War, by which time automobiles were becoming more common. The Chandler Barn was converted to a garage, possibly as late as the 1930s, when two garage door openings were made on the north elevation.

Goodridge Building (W.W. Arcade Ltd.)

Constructed 1911–12
9696–9698 Jasper Avenue
Designated Municipal Historic
Resource May 2000

The Goodridge Building is a well-designed and nicely detailed early example of a commercial building in Edmonton at the turn of the twentieth century. It has been a landmark at the key intersection of Jasper Avenue and Namayo Avenue since the eastern section of Jasper Avenue became the main commercial core of Edmonton.

The design is an elaboration of the Edwardian Age Commercial Style exemplified by many two- to four-storey buildings of the period. The use of pilasters to emphasize the end bays is inspired by the Beaux Arts classicism popular at the time. This tendency to place an emphasis on the end bays is seen in larger scale in John K. Dow's McLeod Building (1913–14) and in a much grander way – using columns, pilasters and/or rusticated blocks with an accented central portion – in the monumental Beaux Arts Legislative Building (designed by A. M. Jeffers, 1907–13). While the Goodridge Block had none of the size, scale or pretension of these buildings, Barnes was making reference to the most advanced compositional tendencies of his time.

The Goodridge Building's classical commercial design and fine brick construction set the architectural tone for the block, and its design was soon mirrored by two other buildings, the Brown Block (designed by James Henderson, 1911–12, and later known as the Brighton Block) and the additions to the Pendennis Hotel (designed by Lang, Major and Company, 1912).

Leonard Angus Goodridge, son of early Edmonton hotelier and alderman James Goodridge, developed the Goodridge Building. Title to the property was registered with Susan Goodridge, James's widow, and when she died in 1907, the title passed to her son Leonard. Leonard Goodridge also owned Jasper House and the Gem Theatre, which he managed until 1957.

In 1910 Leonard Goodridge sold Jasper House to acquire capital to develop his new building immediately to the west on Jasper Avenue. Construction on the Goodridge Block began in the late summer of 1911.

Robert Percy Barnes (1859–1926) was selected as the architect of the Goodridge Block. Barnes was born in London, England, and practised architecture there from 1878 to 1888. After immigrating to Canada in 1888, he worked as an architect in Montreal until 1905, at which time he moved west and settled in Edmonton, where he later went into partnership with Charles Lionel Gibbs (1877–1934). Barnes is credited with having been the founder of the Alberta Association of Architects, established in 1906, and he served as association president in 1909. In 1921 he resigned his seat on the AAA Council in anticipation of moving to Victoria, British Columbia. Besides the Goodridge Block, Barnes was responsible for the design of the Buena Vista Apartments (with Gibbs, 1913) and the Blowey-Henry Block (date unknown, destroyed by fire circa 1948).

The general contractor for the Goodridge Building was the local company of Nesbitt and Miller. Excavation for the new building caused the rear wing of Jasper House to begin to sink, and it nearly collapsed. But Jasper House was saved, and construction continued on the new building.

In 1930 the W.W. Sales hardware business opened in the building under the management of Samuel Peter Wilson. After the new owners, the Ainslie brothers, changed the name in 1942, the location was known to generations of Edmontonians as W.W. Arcade.

Substantial changes were made to the building during a renovation in 1967 when a new storefront was installed, the east wall was rebuilt and the roof replaced.

A FRIENDLY INVASION TRANSFORMS
EDMONTON 1939-1945

When a German submarine torpedoed the British passenger liner SS Athenia on September 3, 1939, the twenty names on the passenger list from Edmonton and northern Alberta brought the outbreak of the Second World War home quickly.

Life soon became directed towards the war effort, and the Prince of Wales Armouries once again became the heart of the city as a makeshift community of tents and barracks sprang up outside its brick walls.

Alberta's contribution to the war was significant. Albertans served in every theatre of war in such distinguished units as The Loyal Edmonton Regiment. Of the 50,844 Albertans to serve in the Royal Canadian Army, many paid the supreme sacrifice or were wounded. A surprising 22 per cent of the Royal Canadian Navy was recruited from the Prairies during the war. In Edmonton, HMCS Nonsuch recruited 3,588 sailors, while many others enlisted in the Merchant Marine or the Royal Navy. Alberta also contributed

◀ *Lend-Lease C-47s and Airacobras at Edmonton Airport awaiting delivery to Russia.* 102A

19,499 men and women to the Royal Canadian Air Force (RCAF), while the RCAF (Women's Division) recruited additional provincial women into its ranks.

Although Edmonton was far from the major theatres of war, it nevertheless played a significant role in the global air war and continental defence. The most immediately visible effect of the war came with the British Commonwealth Air Training Plan facilities hastily constructed throughout Alberta to provide the technicians and aircrews needed for the Allied air forces. An air observer school and elementary flying training school were established in Edmonton. Aircraft Repair Ltd., later to become Northwest Industries, fixed up Allied planes damaged during the war, employing many Edmonton men and women.

The federal government took over control of the city's airport, Blatchford Field, which was rapidly expanded to serve the thousands of Lend-Lease fighters and bombers being ferried to the aid of the Russians through the Northwest Staging Route. The Soviet red star became a familiar sight in Edmonton skies. On one June day in 1942, 500 aircraft were ferried through Blatchford Field. On another memorable day, 860 planes passed through, making Edmonton the busiest airport on the continent. The intense air traffic pushed the facility beyond its capacity, and in September 1944, the Namao Airport opened, becoming the largest in North America at the time. Technology and facilities developed during the war left a lasting influence upon the city.

In addition to the British Commonwealth Air Training Plan, the "friendly invasion" of American construction and service

personnel following the Japanese attack on Pearl Harbor on December 7, 1941, had a massive impact on many parts of Alberta. This was especially true of Edmonton, which became the supply, communications and transportation centre for the Alaska Highway and Canol Pipeline projects. Edmonton truly lived up to its moniker of Gateway to the North as armies of workers were funnelled through on their way to Alaska. During peak activity, over thirty-three thousand Americans were in Alberta, north-eastern British Columbia, and the Yukon Territory. When a terrible blizzard hit the city in November 1942, the "Yanks" turned out to help clear the city's streets.

The social and economic impact of the war on the city was quite striking. Popular culture changed in Edmonton between 1939 and 1945, and these changes were accelerated during the American "occupation" of 1942–45. Religion seemed to play an even deeper role on the home front, while American cultural influences grew more pronounced, partly through the demand among U.S. military personnel and employees of construction companies like Bechtel. Many young men who were in the city training at the British Commonwealth Air Training Plan crowded the local cafés and dance floors, jitterbugging and swinging to the music of Benny Goodman, Glenn Miller and others. Friendships were

forged, and romance flourished despite the disapproval of the military authorities.

As the war progressed, housing shortages rapidly turned from inconvenient to acute when the sudden flood of servicemen and women, American construction workers and Albertans arrived in the city to work in wartime industries. Every spare room was let out, university residences became barracks for airmen, and ramshackle, substandard dwellings sprang up. The trend to renovate and subdivide buildings to allow more tenants – which had begun during the 1930s – accelerated during the war. Wartime housing created distinctive and uniform neighbourhoods of small houses, typically bungalows, near the airport, military installations and armouries.

▲ *The first parade at the American base in September 1944.* 104A

Close to 10 per cent of Canada's population of just over eleven million served in uniform between 1939 and 1945. Countless others served on the home front in farm fields, munitions factories and volunteer war services. By the end of the war the Royal Canadian Air Force (RCAF) was one of the largest air forces in the world, with personnel numbering over a quarter million, sufficient to operate the entire No. 6 Bomber Group. In March 1944, RCAF 418 Squadron, the highest-scoring command by the end of the war, was adopted as the City of Edmonton Squadron. To commemorate the event, Flying Officer "Lefty" Miller, once a delivery boy for the Edmonton Journal, dropped a copy of the newspaper

Edmonton Mayor John Fry visits a U.S. air base in Alaska, April 1944.
105A

from his aircraft on a raid over Kassel, Germany. Most noted for flying dangerous intruder missions over enemy territory in the legendary de Havilland Mosquito fighter-bomber, the City of Edmonton Squadron destroyed 177 enemy aircraft, damaged 103 and shot down 80 V-1 rockets.

During the Second World War, the Royal Canadian Navy became the fourth-largest in the world as it provided the corvettes and frigates to protect convoys in the Battle of the Atlantic. The Royal Canadian Army distinguished itself from Dieppe to Normandy in France, from the Scheldt Estuary in Belgium and the Netherlands to Ortona in Italy. The British Commonwealth Air Training Plan has been judged by many historians to be the single greatest Canadian contribution to the Allied

victory. Edmontonians participated in all these campaigns with distinction.

Victory in Europe Day (VE Day) on May 8, 1945, and Victory over Japan Day (VJ Day) on August 15, 1945, marked the formal end of hostilities in the European and Pacific wars. During that spring and summer, the growing realization that the world had been fundamentally changed swept through the global community. Shock at the atomic bomb attacks on Hiroshima and Nagasaki, revelations of the genocide occurring in the death camps of Eastern Europe, the horrendous casualty lists and the massive dispersal of populations, all brought home the brutal nature of modern warfare. At the same time, a sense of euphoria and optimism found expression among the returning veterans

as they turned their energy toward postwar reconstruction and civil re-establishment.

Mayor John Fry had ably presided over eight years of profound change to his city between 1938 and 1945.

The city would face the challenges of a transformed world after the war as it had a generation before.

The look of the city also began to change here and there. Continental influences were felt in urban design and architectural innovations. The seeds of the postwar suburbs already sown by the proliferating radial railway lines and transit between the wars, were nurtured by the demands of a booming wartime economy. Internal pressure pushed the boundaries of the city from the core,

▲ *Blatchford Field would soon become a major airport hub for WWII supplies to Russia.* 106A

▶ *Victory in Europe Day was marked by an enormous one-word headline in the Edmonton Bulletin in May 1945.* 106B

and American-influenced bungalows began to reappear in more numbers. The rigid grid layout of the city also began to break down in the layout of streets.

During the war years, the city had grown rapidly and had been drawn into the continental and international political and economic world. The wartime search for strategic reserves of oil would soon pay off, and Edmonton would enter a new era of prosperity.

Hangar No. 14

Constructed 1942
11410 Kingsway Avenue
Designated Provincial Historic
Resource July 2000
Designated Municipal Historic
Resource August 2004

Hangar No. 14 is an immense, flat-roofed wooden aircraft hangar on the north side of Kingsway Avenue, adjacent to the Edmonton City Centre Airport, which is soon to be closed and redeveloped. This arresting structure is a rare surviving example of the hangars built in Canada under the British Commonwealth Air Training Plan during the Second World War. Such hangars were of standard design, but could be doubled in size depending on the need of the training school; Hangar No. 14 is the only example of the expanded version known to survive in Canada. Hangar No. 14 primarily served as a supply, staging, training and repair centre for Air Observers School No. 2.

The British Commonwealth Air Training Plan trained Allied pilots, navigators and other aircrew in Canada for duty overseas. The Canadian Prairies – with their low population density, big skies and clear weather – were considered ideal for flight schools. Edmonton was chosen as the location for an initial training school, an elementary flying training school and an air observers school in the Regional Training Command.

President Franklin Delano Roosevelt called the British Commonwealth Air Training Plan "the aerodrome of democracy" for its role in quickly training thousands of Commonwealth aircrew desperately needed to fight the air war in the skies over Europe. The story of Hanger No. 14 is closely associated with the career of pioneer aviator W. R. "Wop" May, who commanded Air Observers School No. 2 stationed at the hanger.

Notoriety seemed to follow Wop May's every move. While serving as a novice in the Royal Flying Corps during the First World War, May was pursued by Manfred von Richthofen, the infamous Red Baron. Flying at treetop height, Germany's most-feared fighter pilot was shot from the sky, presumably by ground fire.

By the end of the war, May had shot down thirteen enemy aircraft and had been

awarded the Distinguished Flying Cross.

Back in Edmonton after the war, Wop May joined the select fraternity of famous bush pilots who opened up the Canadian North when he established the city's first commercial air service and opened Canada's first "air harbour."

In 1928, May's daring was put to the test when, with temperatures plunging to -40° C, he flew vaccine desperately needed to control a diphtheria outbreak at Little Red River, Alberta. Four years later, from the cockpit of his Bellanca monoplane, May participated in the hunt for Albert Johnson, the Mad Trapper of Rat River, who was wanted for the murder of RCMP Constable Spike Millen.

In 1957, Hanger No. 14 became the official home of Edmonton's 418 Squadron after its return from Europe. Today it houses the Edmonton Aviation Heritage Centre, which features a large number of restored and vintage aircraft. Hangar No. 14 possesses an international significance uncommon in Alberta structures because of its role in the British Commonwealth Air Training Plan. It also serves to remind Edmontonians of the city's role as a transportation hub in the development of Canada's North and West.

▲ 109A

Hudson's Bay Company Store

Constructed 1940, Renovated 1954
103rd Street and Jasper Avenue
Designated Municipal Historic
Resource September 1989

The Hudson's Bay Company was a significant and formative influence on the history of Rupert's Land and the Northwest Territories for close to two centuries before the transfer of their trading territory to the Canadian government in 1870. The company brought the first European presence to the Edmonton area in 1795. The bas-relief figures above the entrances of the Hudson's Bay Company department store building on Jasper Avenue commemorate that history.

Hudson's Bay Company stores existed at the present location for some time. The first section of the present structure was built in 1940 by the contractor J. R. McIntyre to plans drawn by the prominent Edmonton architects Magoon and MacDonald. Architects Moody and Moore designed an addition in 1954, while later that year Dewar, Stevenson and Stanley designed the addition of the upper floor that was constructed by C. H. Whitham.

This building is one of Edmonton's most important examples of Moderne Architecture. The site has been redeveloped as a downtown campus for the University of Alberta.

Garneau Theatre
Constructed 1940
8708 109th Street
Designated Municipal Historic
Resource October 2009

The Garneau Theatre is significant for its Art Deco Style, its association with suburbanization in Edmonton after the Second World War, and its status as an Edmonton landmark. It has always been a combined theatre and commercial retail structure, remarkable for its two-tone brown brick, distinctive stucco marquee and one-storey retail portion. The Garneau Theatre, built in 1940, is situated on a prominent corner location at 109th Street and 87th Avenue, immediately south of the historic High Level Bridge in the Garneau neighbourhood. The High Level Bridge was known as the beginning of the Alaska Highway during construction in 1942 and 1943. The Garneau Theatre remains a local landmark due to its conspicuous location on the arterial 109th Street, and its prominent marquee with vertically stacked neon letters reading "GARNEAU" and ladder, designed to attract maximum attention.

The Garneau Theatre is a significant example of Art Deco Style in Edmonton. The terms Moderne, Modernistic and Streamlined Moderne are also used to describe this style. Whatever it may be called, this was an important early stage in the international evolution of modern architecture. The modernism of the Garneau is found in its strongly stated rectilinearity, the use of colour and geometric decoration rather than historical ornamentation and the use of unadorned materials. These stylistic features reflect the work of its architect William G. Blakey, an architect of considerable importance in Edmonton. Other buildings by Blakey include the Masonic Temple, Christ Church, the west wing of the Glenrose Hospital, the Roxy Theatre and his own house, the William Blakey Residence.

In 1942 a rooftop penthouse, designed by prominent local architectural firm Rule Wynn Rule, was built containing a fan room and lounge area. The Garneau Theatre compares well with most of the good Art Deco theatres built across Canada during this period.

The Garneau is valued as an early suburban movie theatre, illustrating the demographic shift to the suburbs and is considered the second of Edmonton's neighbourhood theatres, after the Roxy Theatre, which was built in 1938 at 124th Street and 107th Avenue. The Garneau is one of the few surviving suburban theatres in Edmonton dating from the Second World War.

▲ 111A
▲ 111B

Arndt's Machine Shop

Constructed 1945
10130 81st Avenue
Designated Municipal Historic
Resource May 2009

Arndt's Machine Shop, located in the Ritchie neighbourhood, represents a type of commercial structure typical of the wartime and postwar boom during the 1940s. It is a single-storey building with a corrugated "Quonset style" steel barrel roof, the bowed parapet characterized by a coping block and large, square-corner pilasters on the front façade with square caps and alternating stucco finishes, seen on many other businesses built during that decade, and a central front entrance and textured stucco finish with a wide band of smooth stucco near the base of the building. Arndt's

Machine Shop is especially interesting for its modern commercial design.

Ted Arndt opened a blacksmith shop at this location in 1928 and is believed to have constructed this building to replace the original structure during the mid-1940s. By the 1950s his business had become Arndt's Machine Shop. The business would have benefited from its proximity to the railway and the increased industrial development that occurred in the corridor adjacent to the tracks after the war and the 1947 discovery of oil in Alberta. The change from blacksmith to machinist reflects a broader shift from the last vestiges of the horse-drawn age in Edmonton and its agricultural hinterland, to the increasing mechanization that characterized the city during the rapid urban growth resulting from oil prosperity.

Arndt's Machine Shop is a valued heritage resource due to its modern commercial design. The bowed parapet and square pilasters at the corners conceal the corrugated steel barrel roof and are indicative of a modern variation on the commercial boom-town front design popular at the turn of the century. The slightly textured white stucco finish is typical of these modern commercial structures. Arndt's Machine Shop is one of several modern light-industrial buildings on this block and makes a significant contribution to the character of the Heritage area on this block.

OIL! RECOVERY AND GROWTH
1945-1959

When the veterans came back to civvy street after the war, they wanted to get jobs, build homes, drive cars and make babies.

In the decade between 1947 and 1957 Edmonton's population and average personal income doubled. Between 1947 and 1960, seven annexations were added to Edmonton, including Hardisty, Coronet and Gold Bar. As new districts were amalgamated by the city, services struggled to keep pace with the rapid development. Many streets and sidewalks remained unpaved for some time in the suburban sprawl moving rapidly from the city centre. Though the Hotel Macdonald still dominated the river valley skyline during the 1950s, an annex would be built just east of the hotel, its modern lines described by local wits as "the box the hotel came in." Beneath the annex, the first underground parking lot soon opened to accommodate the downtown traffic of the bustling postwar economy.

◄ *Edmonton City Hall under construction in 1956.* 112A

The discovery of oil on February 13, 1947, ushered in Edmonton's long-awaited second boom. When Imperial Oil Leduc #1 blew in amidst much fanfare, it set in motion developments continuing to this day. In 1948 the first oil refinery was raised in Clover Bar. It was the same old Norman Wells refinery that had first been shipped north during the wartime Canol Pipeline project, but it was a start. British-American and McColl-Frontenac soon followed. In 1950 the first interprovincial oil pipeline connected Edmonton to the Ontario markets.

In 1947 the first mercury-vapour streetlights in the country pushed back the prairie night from Edmonton streets. In that same year, British-born Noel Dant became the first town planner, leaving his mark in the traffic circles, curbs, crescents, cul-de-sacs and service roads that broke up the old rectilinear grid pattern that had characterized Edmonton's earlier development. In 1949 the city adopted a new crest with the motto "Industry Integrity Progress." The new crest replaced the old wheat sheaf and stressed Edmonton's new industrial aspirations.

When Princess Elizabeth and Prince Philip visited the city in October 1951, they encountered a bustling resource-frontier city bursting with energy and confidence. Many Edmontonians were able to watch the event on the wonderful new medium of television. Kids loved the Noon Show, while their mothers were enamoured of Laura Lindsay, two locally produced shows aired live on CFRN-TV.

By 1956 Edmonton and Calgary shared the distinction of being the fastest-growing cities in Canada. Many new public

▲ *Gold Bar Farm before the First World War. In 1958, these buildings would be engulfed by Maclab Enterprises residential developments.* 114A

buildings appeared, including municipal and provincial government services buildings, expansion at the University of Alberta and the new Federal Building. A striking new City Hall was opened in 1957, as was the Northern Alberta Jubilee Auditorium, belatedly celebrating the Golden Jubilee of Alberta. The city sought a new, modern look expressed in International architecture, ranch houses and Arborite™. Innovative builders such as Clifford E. Lee and Merrill Muttart pioneered prefabricated homes and drywall

construction. New architectural theory, which rejected the familiar traditional forms, began to dominate the new buildings appearing throughout the suburbs and commercial districts of Edmonton. It was as though the city, having survived decades of stagnation, depression and war, had emerged into the modern world. A war had been won, young men and women were returning to a normal life of work, raising families and buying comfortable homes. Natural resources and industry pointed the way to the future, and many of their offices and warehouses assumed that forward-looking aspect, which was progressive, international and modern.

William Hawrelak was first elected to the mayoralty in November 1951 and ended his first period in office when he resigned on September 9, 1959. Hawrelak was a successful businessman and seemed to many admirers to fit the spirit of the times. Among Mayor Hawrelak's initiatives was promotion of the new Edmonton International Airport, which began development in 1957. Max Ward launched Wardair in 1953, and jetliners were soon a common feature in the skies above the city. Above all, Edmontonians loved their cars. By 1956 Waterloo Motors led all the North American dealers in sales. The movies and cars came together in 1949 when the Starlight Drive-In theatre opened. "Bring the family … come dressed as you please … enjoy a good show in the comfort and privacy of your own car," touted an advertising feature in the Edmonton Journal. Others soon followed, making Edmonton what some proclaimed as the drive-in-theatre capital of the world.

In 1949 the Low Level Bridge was twinned to speed traffic across the North Saskatchewan River. Strathearn Heights and the Bel-Air Apartments defined a new lifestyle as people flocked to the city, raising their new families in moderately priced accommodation. Diners, groceterias, shopping centres and parking lots began to define the suburbs. The Westmount Shopping Centre became the first in

Edmonton in August 1955, following the opening of the Groat Bridge.

Waterloo Motors supported the Edmonton Mercurys, who won the World Hockey Championship in 1950. When the Mercurys won the Olympic gold medal in 1952, a half-day civic holiday was declared. But the Mercurys were not alone. In 1948, The Edmonton Flyers won the Allan Cup and went on to win successive Western Canada Hockey League titles. Half the city population thronged Jasper Avenue to welcome them home after their victory. Skaters such as Doreen McLeod (Ryan) and Pat Gunn thrilled crowds at the Edmonton Gardens. Matt Baldwin won the Macdonald Brier in 1954, 1957 and 1958. When the Edmonton Eskimos launched the first "dynasty" between 1954 and 1956, Normie Kwong, Johnnie Bright and Jackie Parker, the explosive running back, became local heroes.

With development came the disappearance of some icons and landmarks. The old Edmonton Bulletin, for decades the influential voice of Frank Oliver, closed in 1951. The streetcars, "the most northerly system in North America," ended service in September of the same year.

Even the advent of the Cold War could not dampen postwar enthusiasm. While Emergency Measures Organization drills

▲ *A concept of the Civic Square Plan in the late 1950's, illustrating, at the time, what was felt to be a vision for a prosperous modern City.* 115A

alerted schoolchildren to the dangers of the nuclear age, the city became the supply centre for the mines at Uranium City that produced the raw material that fuelled the nuclear age. By the end of the 1950s, Edmonton felt that it was back where it belonged. On top.

Hyndman Residence

Constructed 1946
10123 136th Street
Designated Municipal Historic
Resource July 2004

The Hyndman Residence is an excellent example of the International Style of architecture, incorporating such defining features as a flat roof (usually without any ledge at the roofline), windows set flush with the outer wall, smooth, unornamented wall surfaces with no decorative detailing at the doors or windows, and an asymmetrical façade. The International Style was considered avant-garde, and most notable American examples date from the 1930s. Certain of the more severe International elements later softened into a more widespread expression known as the Contemporary style.

The Hyndman residence was originally clad in wood-lap siding, not typical of the International style, but it was later stuccoed. The house features cantilevered projections, such as the roof over the front door and the upper balcony, that dramatize the non-supporting nature of the walls.

The house was designed by George Heath MacDonald, of MacDonald and MacDonald, one of two local firms that introduced the Modern Movement to Edmonton. The residence was built by A. C. Carlson for Louis Hyndman, his wife

▲ 116A

Muriel, and their two sons, Peter and Lou, Jr. Born in 1904 and raised in Edmonton, Louis D. Hyndman was a prominent lawyer who also served on the Edmonton School Board and was the first chairman of the city's Planning Advisory Committee. He held the position of Master of Chambers of the Alberta Courts from 1960 to 1986. His son Lou was a member of the Legislative Assembly for Glenora before retiring in 1986, at which time he was provincial treasurer in the Lougheed government.

William Blakey Residence
Constructed 1946
13526 101st Avenue
Designated Municipal Historic
Resource July 2007

The William Blakey Residence is a two-storey residence with a flat roof and stucco cladding that occupies a large corner lot in Glenora neighbourhood, and it is significant primarily for its association with prominent local architect William Blakey, and for its International Style. Blakey designed the home and lived in it from its construction in 1946 until 1971. He was one of the longest-practising architects in Edmonton, whose prolific career began with his arrival from England in 1907 until his retirement in 1963. Some of this work was completed in his home studio built above the garage of this residence.

During his career, Blakey had an enormous impact on Edmonton's built landscape, working on many high profile buildings, including the Edmonton Journal Building (1920-1921), the Masonic Temple (1930), the T. Eaton Store (1938), the Roxy Theatre (1938), the Garneau Theatre (1940) and Christ Church (1946). William Blakey was an early proponent of the International Style of architecture in Edmonton, of which his 1946 home remains a good reminder. Blakey began to explore the principles of modern architecture in the mid-1930s, and in 1946 he used the

▲ 117A

construction of his home to demonstrate his ideas. In 1946 he gave four public lectures on modern architecture, advocating for flat roofs and no basements, ideas visible in his newly constructed residence.

The William Blakey Residence is typified by the use of asymmetrical composition, flat roofs with broad overhanging eaves that emphasize the horizontal massing, relatively smooth unornamented wall surfaces, and corner windows with a horizontal compositional emphasis. The International Style of the Blakey Residence was also evident in other homes in the Glenora neighbourhood, including the Hyndman House next door, also built in 1946. Together, these two residences became an architectural curiosity for many Edmontonians.

Edmonton Telephones Building

Constructed 1945–47
10003 102nd Avenue
Designated Municipal Historic
Resource February 1999

The Churchill Wire Centre (formerly the Edmonton Telephones Building) was one of a growing concentration of civic and governmental structures in the heart of Edmonton, including the Court House, the Land Titles Building, the Public Market, the Civic Block, the Post Office and the Canadian National Railway station. The Edmonton Wire Centre set a new, postwar architectural standard for the civic centre with the use of precast concrete floor slabs, an unusual construction technique at the time and the use of white terrazzo exterior cladding, material not often used in this way and rare in Edmonton.

The Edmonton Labour Hall was demolished in 1945 to make way for a new, modern addition to the existing 102nd Avenue telephone building. City architect Max Dewar was in charge of the project, and the contract for construction went to the Bennett and White Construction Company. Building was originally scheduled to commence in May 1945, but difficulties in obtaining materials and labour during the war delayed progress, and excavation did not begin

118A ▶

▲ 119A   ▲ 119B

until August when the war in the Pacific was drawing to a close. Rather than put construction further behind, it was decided to work on the project through the winter. Hoardings of pine boards and tarpaulins were erected, and eight gas furnaces were installed throughout the building to make conditions bearable. In spite of such efforts, the new building did not open until 1947.

By the 1950s it was again necessary to find more space for telephone exchange equipment. The solution was found in remodelling and modernizing the old exchange and adding a four-storey block on the street side in 1958. After this no major additions or alterations were made to the exterior of the telephone building, known by this time as the Churchill Exchange.

Despite many changes to its interior in subsequent years, the centre proved inadequate once again. In 1984–85 it was

vacated and the telephone equipment was removed. The building was later redeveloped and converted into exclusive apartments.

This structure displays many exterior features typical of the Moderne Style. Glass block is used in the ground floor and above both the main and secondary entrances, while chevron motifs decorate black metal panels separating the main floor windows from the upper floor windows. The latter, arranged in pairs and inset slightly from the plane of the façade, have metal frames with only horizontal mullions. Stylized dentils are found above the second-floor windows, and columns are suggested by vertical flutes in the cast-terrazzo panels making up the upper part of the façade.

Geometric figures such as hexagons and circles are used in the parapet. Reflective materials, mirror-like polished black granite, for example, are used to face the

ground floor, and stainless steel is employed on the entrance doors and doorframes.

The main entrance is set at an angle into the corner of the building and faces directly onto Churchill Square, which was originally occupied by the Stevenson's Furniture Building, also designed in Moderne Style. Two original light fixtures of metal and glass, which continue the geometric motif of the decorative program, flank the main entrance. Above the main entrance is an engraving of a winged Mercury-like figure standing on a globe and holding a bundle of cables in its right hand and a number of lightning bolts in its left hand.

Canadian Imperial Bank of Commerce Building
(Imperial Bank of Canada)
Constructed 1950
9990 Jasper Avenue
Designated Municipal Historic
Resource March 2004

The Imperial Bank of Canada, the first chartered bank in Edmonton, was important to the development of Edmonton. This particular building was the fourth downtown building used by the Imperial Bank and the third on this site.

No first generation bank buildings remain downtown, although several second generation bank and trust company buildings from the pre-First World War boom remain standing.

Rule Wynn Rule, the most important architects of the early "modern" era in Alberta, were the local supervising architects for this building. The nominal architect, A. J. Everett, the staff architect of the Imperial Bank of Canada, designed the building in an early example of Modern Classicism, a conservative approach to modernist architecture. Steel-frame construction with stone-and-glass exterior curtain walls characterize the building, and it is presumed to be an early example of the technique for Edmonton. The materials became commonplace later in the 1950s.

▲   120A

The building has undergone little change. Other than some alterations to private offices on the upper floors and the installation of partitions for automatic banking machines, virtually all of the original partitions and finishes remain unaltered.

Now known as the World Trade Centre, this striking building remains a conspicuous downtown landmark at the most familiar intersection on Jasper Avenue.

Phillips Building

Constructed 1912 Renovated 1956
10169 104th Street
Designated Municipal Historic
Resource August 2001

The exterior façade of the Phillips Building was re-clad with modern materials in 1956, although the original façade remains intact under the renovations. At the same time the façade was redesigned to make it appear more "modern," in accord with the prevailing atmosphere of Edmonton's postwar prosperity. Such renovations have been common in the city, especially during the 1920s and 1930s.

The Phillips Building was designed in the Commercial Style with the generous windows typical of the style. Five storeys high and eight bays wide, with walls of red brick, it originally had a twenty-two-foot-wide arcade running through its length, making it a first of its kind in Edmonton.

Designed and built for owners N. W. Purcell and J. G. Kelly, it used the latest technology, such as fireproof doors and windows, and was one of the first completely fireproof buildings in Edmonton. It was originally leased to the Western Cartage Company as a storage warehouse.

The Phillips Building was built during the great economic boom preceding the First World War, a time when Edmonton was coming into its own as a distribution centre for the surrounding agricultural settlements and as a gateway to the Canadian North. Manufactured goods were stored here awaiting shipment to destinations all over the West and North.

The 104th Street façade reveals the original 1912 face with thirty-two double-hung wooden windows featuring cast-stone sills and headers, brick corbelling above the windows on the fifth floor, period reproductions of the metal cornice work at the upper parapet level, and an intermediate-level faux-stone base at the storefront level with similar surrounds at the four entrances at ground level, and period reproductions of the storefronts and four entrances.

121A ▶

St. Francis of Assisi Friary/ St. Anthony's College

Constructed 1925,
Rebuilt 1931, 1946
6770 129th Avenue
Designated Municipal Historic
Resource March 2006

St. Francis of Assisi Friary/St. Anthony's College is a fine example of the Gothic Revival style of architecture. The original structure is a basic rectangular brick building. However, the 1931 addition was designed in the Gothic Revival style. The south-facing front has an asymmetrical projected entry with a stepped parapet and niche containing a religious statue. It also features pointed-arch windows with keystones on the first floor.

The simple original building was built in 1925 on a concrete foundation with three floors of poured-in-place concrete structural floors supported on the exterior walls and interior bearing walls. The exterior walls consist of structural clay tile clad with red-brown brick. The interior bearing walls also consist of structural clay tile.

The architect of the 1925 building is not recorded, although it is known that the builder was J. P. Desrochers Company Ltd. Edward Underwood was the architect of the 1931 addition, and the builder was once again J. P. Desrochers. Both Underwood and Desrochers were prominent in the construction of churches and other buildings during the 1920s and 1930s for the Archdiocese of Edmonton. Both also were responsible for the design and construction of the Oblates Maison Provinciale. The 1946 gym addition was designed by George Heath MacDonald and built by Mill and Olsen.

The history of the St. Francis of Assisi Church and St. Anthony's College begins with the arrival of the industrial growth stimulated by the arrival of Canadian Northern Railway in Edmonton in 1905. The neighbourhood was called Packingtown because of the establishment of Swift's Canadian Company's packing plant located at Fort Road and 66th Street. A visible reminder of this history is the landmark Canada Packers Chimney Stack still standing in the area. With industry came a growing population and the need for missionaries.

Encouraged by the Very Reverend Father Coulombe Dryer and Bishop Emile J. Legal of Saint Albert, the Franciscans came west to establish a mission in the Edmonton area. In June 1909 the first temporary monastery for the Franciscan Friars was built on the present site of the St. Francis of Assisi Friary. The first missionaries were Father Boniface

Heidmeyer and Brother Andrew Chevalier. Construction began on a permanent friary soon after the completion of the temporary structure, and it was considered sufficiently complete to move into by October 1909. The friary was the first permanent foundation of the Franciscan Apostolate in Western Canada and was the office of the Major Superior of the Ecclesiastic Province of Christ the King (an area stretching from the Ontario–Manitoba border to Vancouver Island). In 1912 the first St. Francis of Assisi Church was completed and officially blessed.

By the early 1920s the Franciscans obtained permission from Archbishop H. J. O'Leary of Edmonton to open a Seraphic College for Franciscan Vocations. The cornerstone of the first building was laid on May 17, 1925, and was completed in September.

▲ 125A

Richard Wallace Residence

Constructed circa 1923
10950 81st Street
Designated Municipal Historic
Resource August 2003

The Richard Wallace Residence is a typical Craftsman residence with a front gable roof and a porch having notable eave overhangs, exposed braces and rafters. The simple little house is clad in timber siding and clapboard, and has wooden shingles.

Tapered columns sitting on a closed porch railing support the low-pitched roof. The gable end is sided with shingles and sits on a heavy decorative timber board lintel. Three decorative knee-brace brackets support the roof overhang, two attached to the columns.

Robert Aitchison, a photographer, was the home's first occupant, but from 1925 to 1943 Richard Wallace, Registrar, Sheriff and Clerk of the Supreme Court, lived here.

William Noble, Manager of the School Book Branch, Alberta Department of Education, then occupied the house from 1944 to 1953.

This type of modest residence is increasingly being valued by heritage preservationists and is being found on the designation lists usually reserved in the past only for grand mansions. It reflects the importance of ordinary people who played a part in our civic growth and now take their place in our civic heritage.

◄ 124A

THE EXUBERANT DECADE
1960-1969

The Sixties experienced the full impact of the postwar baby boom.

Students flooded the schools and universities and became more active in politics. Edmonton struggled to accommodate the needs of the burgeoning school population. New schools and temporary portables were the most visible responses to the demand, but the city also advanced experimental and progressive school systems that remained at the forefront of North American education. In October 1962 the Northern Alberta Institute of Technology opened, signalling a renewed focus on technical education.

Edmonton became a more cosmopolitan urban centre with each passing year, and the appearance of the city was transformed as high-rise apartments rose along the river valley and suburbs spread out in all directions. In 1961 the city annexed

◀ *The Caravan Motor Hotel in 1964, since renamed, located on 100 Avenue East of 105 Street.* 126A

Beverly, which had existed as a separate community for forty-eight years, and in 1963, the City of Jasper Place was annexed.

Mayor Elmer Roper and City Council renewed a vision for the city centre when they approved plans to revitalize the urban core in June 1962. A city square was to be essential to the plan. In March 1965 Sir Winston Churchill Square was named for the great wartime leader, who died that year. Also in 1965, the Edmonton Art Gallery opened, and in 1966 the CN Tower anchored the downtown at its northern end. A modern downtown library was planned to commemorate the Canadian centennial. The square was beginning to take its present shape as new architectural forms began to change the face of Edmonton. Bold functional design was becoming the hallmark of the reinvigorated city centre.

Queen Elizabeth II and Prince Philip visited the city in 1959. In September 1960 Edmonton opened the first municipally owned planetarium in Canada, named the Queen Elizabeth II Planetarium to commemorate the first visit of the new monarch.

The International Airport officially opened in 1960. Its modern buildings and impressive mural by Jack Shadbolt, commemorating the early history of Edmonton aviation, indicated a desire to move into the international community.

In 1967 Great Canadian Oil Sands began production of synthetic crude oil near Fort McMurray, heralding a new era in resource development for Edmonton. In the coming decades, the oil sands would fulfil the dreams of pioneers such as S. C. Ells and Dr. Karl Clark, and would become increasingly

▲ *The Queen Elizabeth II Planetarium. Opened in 1960 as Canada's first municipally owned planetarium.* 128A

▲ *Churchill Square looking northwest towards Centennial Place, the Avord Arms and the CN Tower towering over City Hall in December 1967.* 128B

important in supplying the world's growing demand for fossil fuels. Clare Drake, coach of the University of Alberta Golden Bears hockey team for twenty-eight years, exemplified the spirit of sport throughout the decade. His career total of 697 wins and 37 ties is the best record in intercollegiate hockey in North America. Drake coached six national championship teams and won sixteen Canada West titles. He also coached university football during the decade and won the championship in 1967, making him the only coach in Canadian Inter-University Athletic Union history to win championships in two sports.

As Canada's centennial drew near, the celebration of history and culture were back on the agenda. The first Klondike Days opened in July 1962 and marked every July until 2006. The Provincial Museum of Alberta, renamed the Royal Alberta Museum to commemorate another royal visit in 2005, opened its doors to the public in 1967, the national centennial year.

The Edmonton Professional Opera Association arrived on the scene in 1963. In 1964 the first Citadel Theatre, founded by Joe Shoctor, opened in the old Salvation Army Citadel. Ruth Carse established the Alberta Ballet Company in 1966, and later the Alberta Ballet School. Marek Jablonski brought the name of his home city to the world as he achieved international fame as a brilliant concert pianist.

The built heritage of the city came under increasing pressure during the 1960s. The economic growth spurred a boom in the cultural, sporting and social life of the city. Welcome though these changes were, the vision of a new city exacted a price. Many familiar and historically and architecturally noteworthy buildings began to disappear under the wrecking ball in the name of progress.

As Edmonton's skyline and residential districts underwent a radical transformation, Edmontonians still held a place in their heart for some of their cherished personalities. The raucous voice of Pete Jamieson, our self-appointed town crier since 1935, was still heard. Sam

▲ *Victoria High School, as it appeared in 1962, was another casualty of the growth period that undervalued the importance of heritage in its environment.* 129A

▲ *The downtown Post Office Building, another later casualty of the City's growth at the time.* 129B

Cherniak, a downtown fixture since 1938, still sold peanuts from his cart which stood near the old Tegler Building.

At the same time that the brawny postwar city began to flex its muscles, looking to a brighter future, it seemed to turn its back on the past in some ways. Transportation projects demanded by the new suburbs, road construction through older neighbourhoods and an appetite for new architectural forms led to a devaluation of the character of older, inner-city districts. Grassroots movements began to emerge as a countervailing influence to this overwhelming impulse to recalibrate Edmonton to a faster lifestyle, one more attuned to the automobile and the kind of city it demands.

Valleyview Manor

Constructed 1960
12207 Jasper Avenue
Designated Municipal Historic
Resource November 2010

Valleyview Manor is an eight-storey apartment building containing 45 units constructed during 1960 and 1961, located on the south side of Jasper Avenue overlooking the North Saskatchewan River Valley in the Oliver neighbourhood. Valleyview Manor is associated with the Winspear family and was designed by prominent local architectural firm Rule Wynn Rule.

Valleyview Manor is one of Edmonton's first high-rise apartment buildings and represents the beginning of a cultural shift from traditional, single family home ownership to high-quality, rental accommodation designed for the professional white-collar market. The scale and height of the building were important in the developing skyline of Edmonton and mark a transition from earlier low-scale development to imposing projects that came to be undertaken in the 1970s and 1980s. The construction of these new apartment buildings heralded a momentous change in the skyline of Edmonton that took advantage of the natural setting of the river valley and provided an alternative

130A ▶

urban lifestyle for its inhabitants. Valleyview Manor was among the first new apartments along Jasper Avenue and represents an important change in postwar Edmonton.

Valleyview Manor is also associated with the prominent Winspear family. Francis Winspear was a major investor in the building and, upon its completion, lived with his wife Bess in an enlarged three-bedroom apartment on the top floor. Francis Winspear is considered synonymous with business acumen, philanthropy and the arts in Edmonton, and during his 60-year business career was president and CEO of 19 companies in a range of industries, including oil, steel, lumber, mining, aircraft and airlines, textiles, finance and real estate development. He taught accounting for 20 years at the University of Alberta and served as director of the University's School of Commerce, and dean of the Business School. Francis Winspear was a fellow of the Royal Society for the Encouragement of the Arts and helped found the Edmonton Symphony Orchestra and the Edmonton Opera. He was the recipient of numerous awards of recognition, including Officer of the Order of Canada and the Alberta Order of Excellence. After Bess died, Francis in 1980 married the widow Harriet Snowball, who had served as the resident manager of Valleyview Manor since its opening. Harriet Winspear was actively involved in Edmonton's arts community and with

her husband helped the Edmonton Opera achieve national standing, built swimming pools and camps for children, made substantial contributions to scholarships for students at the University of Alberta and made the Edmonton United Way one of the most successful in Canada. She was named a member of the Order of Canada in 2003.

Valleyview Manor was designed by Gordon Wynn, of Rule Wynn Rule, a predominant architectural firm in Alberta that through succession is still in operation today. Rule Wynn Rule were the architects of some of the more notable modern buildings in the province and had a strong sense of style and construction that is evident in Valleyview Manor. The simple form, robust detailing, large fenestration patterns and projecting balconies enable the building to take advantage of its natural setting.

The characteristic yellow-brick cladding with concrete framed construction and projecting balconies makes the Valleyview representative of this important design firm. The ceramic mosaic tile and marble cladding to the lower floor and entrance canopy with domed skylights remain important aspects of the building.

The large spacious apartments and durability of the construction have ensured that the building has remained largely unaltered, and it is a fine example

▲ 131A

of the development that transformed the city. It is unique as being the sole Rule Wynn Rule apartment in Edmonton designed by partner Gordon Wynn.

CONFIDENCE AND PROSPERITY
1970-1979

In 1971 the Progressive Conservatives, under Peter Lougheed, swept to power, ending the Social Credit Party's thirty-six years of continuous rule.

The new provincial government was quick to increase oil royalties, and in 1973 the Organization of Petroleum Exporting Countries (OPEC) suddenly raised oil prices. These two events ensured Edmonton's continued role as the Oil Capital of Canada. Vast developments in the oil sands to the north solidified that role.

Throughout the remainder of the 1970s, Edmonton found itself riding the wave of a superheated economy, attracting thousands of new workers and striving to meet the demands of a burgeoning population. Downtown growth accelerated with the construction of twenty-six high-rise towers.

◀ *Edmonton was poised for its launch into the next buoyant energy-fuelled decade when this image of the downtown was captured in 1970.* A132

In May 1974, Phase I of Edmonton Centre opened to the public, with other buildings following to the west of Churchill Square.

But landmarks familiar to Edmontonians for years were disappearing. The Court House vanished, and the main Post Office was demolished in 1972. The Civic Block also was replaced. Many began to ponder what was being lost, and a heritage preservation movement started to take shape. The Old Strathcona Foundation was established on November 13, 1974, to oppose a planned freeway through Old Strathcona. Men of vision such as Gerry Wright fought to preserve the city's built heritage.

Everything and everybody was on the move. Even the Cenotaph was moved to its present site on Sir Winston Churchill Square. Other landmarks appeared on the square. The

new Law Courts opened in 1972, while the striking Citadel Theatre opened in 1976.

A series of new bridges to handle the growing influx of suburban commuters culminated with the construction of the James Macdonald Bridge, which opened in October 1971. Suburban shopping centres came into their own. In 1970 Southgate Shopping Centre was advertised as the largest west of Toronto. Then, in August 1972, the Londonderry Mall did it one better – or at least bigger. This concentrated form of retail activity rapidly intensified the movement to the suburbs during the 1970s. The little neighbourhood shopping centres located in the middle of the suburbs during the 1950s, gave way to the larger strip malls and finally to the mega malls with vast tracts of parking space. Edmontonians enthusiastically adapted to this new lifestyle and demanded even

more and bigger malls. Why walk to the corner store, or visit Woodward's or Eaton's department stores downtown, when you could drive five miles to a new mall?

Edmonton began to see itself as the City of Champions as the decade progressed. The Edmonton Coliseum (now known as Rexall Place) opened in November 1974 and would become the focus for much of the excitement. Following in the winning tradition of the Edmonton Flyers and the Edmonton Oil Kings, the Alberta Oilers came to town to represent the World Hockey Association in 1972. Renamed the Edmonton Oilers, the team would soon become one of the proudest standard-bearers for the city.

The Edmonton Eskimos, after languishing for some time, burst back onto the scene in 1973, winning an uninterrupted five Grey Cups between 1978 and 1982.

Commonwealth Stadium opened in October 1977, and Edmonton's Light Rapid Transit system, the first of its kind in Canada, began operation in April 1978, ready to carry the throngs of sports fans to the XI Commonwealth Games held from the third to the twelfth of August. The city basked in the international limelight.

◀ *Edmonton House under construction, 1971.* 134A

Diane Jones-Konihowski and John Primrose proved that Edmontonians had the right stuff.

Edmonton prizes its magnificent river valley and its ravines, and in July 1978, in time for the Commonwealth Games, Capital City Recreation Park opened. This ambitious project brought more people into the valley to walk, run, cycle, picnic and play team sports. Already, Mayfair Park, later renamed Hawrelak Park, had opened in 1967 to form the cornerstone of the great project. The deep civic pride of the 1970s had much in common with the first boom that preceded the First World War. Sports, the arts, culture and heritage preservation were the beneficiaries.

▲ *The Light Rail Transit with Commonwealth Stadium in the background, shortly after the opening of both the stadium and the rail service in 1978.* 135A

▶ *The architectural heritage of Edmonton, exemplified by the magnificent Secord Mansion at the corner of 100th Avenue and 105th Street, began to disappear rapidly during the 1970s. An alarmed community began to organize to preserve the remnant. This image was taken from a souvenir album printed in 1914.* 135B

▲ 136A   ▲ 136B

Magrath Mansion

Constructed 1912
6240 Ada Boulevard
Designated Provincial Historic
Resource September 1975

The mansion was built for William J. Magrath, who, with Bidwell A. Holgate, was a founder of the Highlands development. The house was built on sprawling grounds facing the boulevard named for William's wife, Ada.

The Magrath Mansion is distinguished by its massive columns, a colonnade curving around the veranda, and a porte-cochere.

Highlands architect Ernest William Morehouse designed the mansion to set an unprecedented residential standard in Edmonton. To this end, Morehouse used such materials as mahogany, Italian marble, hand-painted silk, linen wallpaper and Bohemian crystal. Cherubs and floral patterns were stencilled on ceiling panels and walls. The mansion also featured central heating, electricity, a basement swimming pool and a telephone in every room.

William Magrath died in 1921, but Ada kept the house until 1933, when it was seized for non-payment of taxes, another victim of the cruel cycles of entrepreneurial feast and famine.

In 1948 the house was purchased by the Ukrainian Catholic Diocese and became the first Edmonton residence to be designated a Provincial Historic Resource.

Rutherford House

Constructed 1911
11153 Saskatchewan Drive
Designated Provincial Historic
Resource June 1979

Rutherford House, an impressive two-storey, red-brick-and-sandstone dwelling, is located on the north side of the University of Alberta campus overlooking the North Saskatchewan River valley. An excellent example of upper-class Edwardian-era domestic architecture, it was designed for Dr. Alexander Cameron Rutherford, the first premier of Alberta, by the Strathcona firm of Arthur G. Wilson and David E. Herrald. The grand project featured Georgian/Jacobethan Revival influences popular in Rutherford's native Ontario. It also incorporated many modern conveniences. It was the Georgian-influenced balcony supported by massive pillars at the entrance that dominated the structure, giving it a virtually unequalled prominence in Edmonton. The fenestration presented Palladian style windows, felt by many to suggest the traditions of the British Empire. A stained-glass skylight illuminated the bifurcated interior staircase. From his front porch, Rutherford enjoyed an unobstructed view of the magnificent North Saskatchewan valley and the Provincial Legislature.

Alexander Rutherford lived here from its completion in 1911 until his death in 1941.

▲ 137A

He named it Achnacarry after the ancestral home of his mother's clan, the Camerons.

As premier between 1905 and 1910, Rutherford and his Liberal government laid the legislative and administrative foundations of the new province. Rutherford took a strong interest in public education and was a powerful influence in establishing the University of Alberta nearby in 1907. While living in Rutherford House, he continued to practise law and was president of the Historical Society

of Alberta from 1919 to 1941, on the University Senate from 1907 to 1927, and university chancellor from 1927 to 1941.

Rutherford House is one of the most impressive examples of domestic architecture in early twentieth-century Alberta. Restoration began in 1971 after a heated protest against its planned demolition, and it was re-opened to the public in 1973.

BOOM AND BUST
1980-1989

The 1980s began with artist Peter Lewis installing the Great Divide Waterfall on the High Level Bridge.

The largest man-made waterfall in the world, it is 7.3 metres higher than Niagara Falls and is operated on special occasions in summer. Constructed to celebrate Alberta's seventy-fifth anniversary, the waterfall is an emblem of a decade of mixed blessings during which Edmonton suffered downturns in the midst of new highs.

The booming 1970s gave way to an economic slump following the failure of the Alsands project in 1982 and a growing malaise following the Gainers strike, the most violent in the city's history. The decade was defined by relatively slow economic progress in many sectors. Still, Phase I of the West Edmonton Mall threw open its doors in September 1981 with Phases II through IV opening in 1983, 1985 and 1999. Boasting some 5.4 million square

◄ *The first Great Divide Waterfall display, 1980.* 138A

feet of space, including the world's largest indoor water park, the mall grew rapidly to become the largest shopping mall and entertainment venue in the world, receiving 22 million visits annually.

In the downtown core, economic decline and the demolition of heritage buildings continued. The Rialto Theatre, the beautiful Art Moderne Eaton's store, the Woolworth's store and the Tegler Building were lost, but the city forged ahead with new architectural landmarks. Peter Hemingway's striking Muttart Conservatory, characterized by its pyramid pavilions, had opened in 1976. It became a distinctive part of the river valley in Cloverdale and prepared the way for other projects with unique designs. The futuristic Edmonton Space Sciences Centre, designed by renowned Alberta architect Douglas Cardinal, opened at Coronation Park on Canada Day 1984. Mayor Terry

Cavanagh proclaimed the old City Hall closed on February 28, 1989, and Edmonton architect Gene Dub was awarded the design contract for the new City Hall that has become a key feature of Churchill Square.

Natural disasters visited the city again. On July 31, 1987, a powerful tornado left a track of destruction as it ploughed across the North Saskatchewan River and through east Edmonton, raking northern and south-eastern neighbourhoods and killing twenty-nine Edmontonians. As a result, the Edmonton Emergency Relief Agency was organized, and sophisticated Doppler technology was installed to forecast such incidents more accurately.

The Walter C. Mackenzie Health Sciences Centre, dedicated to the pursuit of research and health care, opened in September 1986, a sign of the position the city and province

▲ *The Peter Hemingway-designed Coronation Pool in Edmonton's Coronation Park. In 2012 it won the Prix du XXE Siecle Award as a nationally significant building.* 140A

were taking at the forefront of medical research. By the 1980s the University of Alberta Hospitals were renowned for their work in heart and kidney transplants.

Edmonton was now dubbed the Festival City. The first Fringe Theatre project was launched in 1982. Inspired by the great Edinburgh Fringe Festival, the Edmonton Fringe grew to become the largest in North America and a foundation upon which the many subsequent festivals would build.

Visual arts became important in the civic domain. Laurence Decore, mayor from 1983 to 1988, was presented with his new chain of office on May 29, 1986. This

was to be worn at ceremonial functions. Max Podluzny was the designer, and his creation reflected the origins of the city in the fur trade as well as the many military and police units that had served the city.

Edmonton's multicultural roots were celebrated and an increasingly cosmopolitan outlook emerged. On December 5, 1985, Edmonton was twinned with Harbin, in Heilongjiang, China. The following year, 102nd Avenue between 95th and 97th Streets was named Harbin Street, and the Friendship Gate to Chinatown was dedicated on October 24, 1987. Festival '88 – featuring arts, dance, crafts and tours of the Ukrainian Cultural Heritage Village east of the city – commemorated the millennium of Ukrainian Christianity and reminded Edmontonians of the vital role played by Ukrainian Canadians in the settling of central Alberta.

Sports teams and events brought Edmonton fame as the City of Champions. The Edmonton Oilers won five Stanley Cups in 1984, 1985, 1987, 1988 and 1990. The Edmonton Eskimos dynasty won the Grey Cup again in 1987, adding to an impressive record of playoff berths that no North American sports franchise has equalled. Baseball also returned to the city. In 1984 the Edmonton Trappers became the first Canadian club in the Pacific Coast League to win the championship, though the team regrettably left the city in 2003. By 1987 the Trappers had the top ten hitters in the league. Jim Eppard became the first Trapper to gain the Pacific Coast League championship that year.

The XII World Universiade Games in July 1983 galvanized citizens' renowned spirit of volunteerism as Edmonton hosted the first World University Games to be held in North America. The international spotlight

was on the city. Legacies were built, such as the Edmonton Convention Centre and notable sports facilities, which subsequently attracted other venues. The decade confirmed Edmonton as a city of champions and festivals. Civic pride was buoyed again by the achievements of its sportsmen and sportswomen and cultural events.

Pride turned to its built form and the realisation that there was a need to apply better urban design principles to a city living under the stress of growth through boom and bust cycles. Efforts were made to encourage property owners to invest in the more intangible qualities of their buildings and grounds. Incentives were considered to this end for the first time. The City invested in older commercial neighbourhoods, with Old Strathcona leading the way, and supported the Province and preservation groups such as Heritage Canada. Community planning in its broadest sense

▲ *The "City of Edmonton", the first commercial aircraft to fly out of Edmonton, was piloted by Wilfrid Reid "Wop" May in 1919. For many years it was aloft in the lobby of Edmonton's Shaw Conference Centre.* 141A

▲ *The City of Edmonton's 'Space Science Centre' designed by Douglas Cardinal.* 141B

now was being addressed by an inclusive array of stakeholders. Revitalization efforts began to include natural landscaping, hard landscaping, pedestrian-friendly streets, art in public places and interpretive design like the imaginative Heritage Trail. The city, as always, looked to the future, laying the groundwork for the progress that it hoped would come in the 1990s.

LOOKING TO OUR SECOND CENTURY
1990 AND INTO THE 21ST CENTURY

Edmonton entered its tenth decade amid economic recovery from the decline of the oil sector during the 1980s. It would seem a prolonged process to Edmontonians, eager to experience a return to more prosperous times.

Mordecai Richler had once described Edmonton in unflattering terms in a New York Times article in 1985, calling it "a jumble of a used-building lot where the spare office towers and box-shaped apartment buildings and cinder-block motels discarded in the construction of real cities have been abandoned to waste away in the cruel prairie winter." Indeed, things were in a slump, with urban growth seemingly losing its struggle to unimaginative development, although the situation probably was not quite so desperate as Richler suggested. At the same time, Terry Fenton, director of the Edmonton Art Gallery, was promoting Edmonton as "Sculpture City" for its many progressive public statues by artists like Peter Hide. Nevertheless, Mayor Jan Reimer reported

◀ *The new downtown Grant McEwan University campus.* 142A

in 1992 that the city still continued to cope with the effects of a strained economy. "We find ourselves struggling to serve a growing population with a variety of needs, despite cutbacks in [provincial] funding."

As the city prepared for its Biennial Celebration in 1995 things were beginning to look better. The superbly restored Macdonald Hotel had reopened in 1991. The hotel, which for years dominated the river valley skyline and was the pre-eminent hotel in town, once again became the place to meet visiting dignitaries from prime ministers to rock stars such as the Rolling Stones.

The northern focal point of Churchill Square took its final form in 1993 when the magnificent new City Hall opened. Another important addition to cultural activity around the square was the opening

of the Winspear Centre for Music in 1997. Francis Winspear made the project possible through a $6-million donation, the largest single private donation in Canadian history at the time. The Winspear Centre would attract important musicians and performers to the city in the coming years.

Edmonton benefitted when Canadian Forces Base Namao, with its historical roots dating back to the Second World War, was expanded. The new consolidated base grew in 1998 when the Department of Defence reorganized its units, making Namao the foremost base in Western Canada. Shortly thereafter, Edmontonians were reminded of the deep historical connection between the armed forces and the city when in 1999 the Reverend Cyril Martin, an Edmonton veteran, belatedly received at age 99 the Legion of Honour, the

◀ *The Alberta Art Gallery adds new architectural interest to Edmonton's Churchill square.* 144A

highest honour bestowed by France, for service in the First World War.

Edmonton's tenth decade witnessed many tangible signs of growth and development. But the intangible signs of the Edmonton spirit were just as valuable. They could be found in the many ethnic, cultural and artistic groups and individuals who flourished in every corner of the city and brought their vision to Edmontonians and to the broader world.

During the 1990s, Edmonton strengthened its identity as Festival City. The Heritage Festival, established in 1976, was recognized in 1999 by the American Business Association as one of the hundred foremost events in North America. The Edmonton Kiwanis Festival, established in 1908 and the oldest continuing music festival in Canada, continued to grow in prestige. The Works, the largest festival of the visual

arts in North America, continued to build on its mandate to bring art to people in a variety of venues in the downtown and outlying districts. The Jazz City International Music Festival, Symphony Under the Sky, the Edmonton Folk Music Festival and numerous other events filled the streets of the city from spring to fall.

Edmonton continued to witness important sports events. In 1996 Edmonton hosted the World Figure Skating Championships, and in 2003 the Eskimos won another Grey Cup, raising the spirits of the city as they had on previous occasions. The Edmonton Oilers struggled for support following the team's heyday during the 1980s. In 1998 a group of Edmonton business people purchased the team, the first such example of community ownership of a National Hockey League team and a tribute to hockey's deep roots in the city.

One thread runs through the story of our first hundred years: Edmontonians have always helped each other in times of hardship and fortune. Volunteers have emerged to meet every emergency, from flood to tornado. The Edmonton Federation of Community Leagues was an early example of this charitable impulse, and the city exhibits a truly remarkable degree of volunteer spirit. From food banks to international games, from the Fringe to the Works, the city can point with pride to a tradition of its citizens getting behind community events.

Views of Edmonton often are painted in broad strokes, but a closer examination reveals the many detailed portraits of Edmontonians, heralded and unheralded, who have made a difference. Every Edmontonian has his or her own history, a unique story to tell in a unique voice. From its earliest times, the community has

▶ *Edmonton's 3rd City Hall, completed in 1992, provided a public focal point in the City centre.* 145A

gained strength from those who came to build a life and make a future in this city. At first the fur trade brought the Scots, English, French and Métis to the land of the First Nations. Later came the Chinese and the Ukrainians and other east-European immigrants during the early boom years. Then came the Italians, Greeks, Indians and Pakistanis. Today new groups – Vietnamese, Kurds, Mandinka and others – arrive seeking a safe haven in a dangerous world. Every generation has brought new people who have added to the character and heritage of our city.

Throughout its first hundred years, Edmonton has forged a characteristic can-do attitude that has not diminished but increased as the city has grown and become more metropolitan. With such an outlook, Edmonton can look confidently to the next century.

▲ 146A   ▲ 146B

Hotel Macdonald
Constructed 1915
10065 100th Street
Designated Municipal Historic
Resource January 1985

The Hotel Macdonald was designed by the Winnipeg and Montreal architecture firm of Ross and MacFarlane. The façade is finished in Indiana limestone with a copper roof, now blackened with the patina the years have brought. Its interior features steel-frame construction, reinforced concrete flooring, gypsum-rock walls and terra cotta interior partitions.

The original ten-storey hotel had 175 rooms and was built by the Grand Trunk Pacific Railway for the incredible sum at the time of $2.2 million. When it formally opened on July 6, 1915, nearly a year after

the outbreak of the First World War in Europe, a local newspaper observed: "It was perhaps the most brilliant social event in the city's history, for never before has it been possible to carry out a similar function upon so colossal a scale."

Over the years this landmark has come to be known affectionately as the Mac. Setting a new standard in opulent hostelry, the Mac featured the octagonal Palm Room, which later was named the Wedgwood Room because of its groin ceiling with Wedgwood-design plaster reliefs. The rotunda and corridors were paved in Lepanto marble. The two-storey Empire Ballroom occupied the end of the east wing and featured plaster-relief depictions of hunting scenes around the ceiling. The Confederation Room, with its high ceiling and arched doorway to the

south patio where tea was served during the summer months, included a massive painting of the Fathers of Confederation. The 1915 painting by Frederick S. Challener remains where he supervised its installation.

In 1953 a sixteen-storey rectangular wing was added. It was referred to, in a well-worn local joke as "the box the Mac came in." When the Mac closed in 1983 for a restoration, Canadian National Hotels President Donald Gordon announced that the original wing might be replaced by a modern addition to conform to the style of the 1953 tower. Fortunately, better judgement prevailed and the addition was torn down in 1986. Restored to its former glory, the Macdonald reopened to re-establish its place at the centre of the civic cultural life of Edmonton.

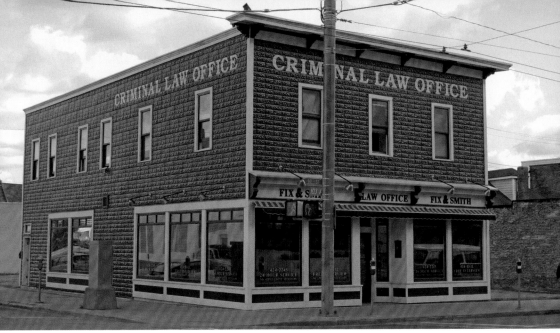

▲ 147A

Kingston Powell Building

Constructed circa 1907
10277 97th Street
Designated Municipal Historic
Resource December 2002

The Kingston Powell Building is typical of boom-town commercial properties built around the turn of the twentieth century. Constructed of timber and entirely clad in metal siding pressed to resemble stone blocks, it is the single surviving example of the hundreds that once lined Namayo Avenue, one of the two principal downtown commercial districts in its day. The front façade at parapet level is capped with a timber decorative cornice detail. Originally there were two commercial frontages, rather than the current single central doorway.

The building was constructed for Kingston

Powell, a prominent and successful local farmer who presumably desired to participate in the financial benefits of the pre-First World War boom and to use it as an investment for his retirement. The first occupants included a typical array of businesses of the period. The building also stands as an excellent example of creative reuse of a heritage property. Today a law practice owns and operates the building.

147B ▶

Hull Block

Constructed 1914
10601–10607 97th Street
Designated Municipal Historic
Resource August 2001
Designated Provincial Historic
Resource August 2003

The Hull Block, the largest and most significant building in Edmonton's historic Chinatown district, continues to play a vital role in the preservation of the streetscape's character. It exhibits distinctive and prominent metal cornices at the parapet level and attractive brick detailing.

By 1909, the Canadian Northern and Grand Trunk Pacific railways were linked to Edmonton, and a large warehouse and industrial district quickly grew up in the downtown's west end near the rails. McCauley attracted working-class immigrants who wanted to be near centres of employment, leading to the emergence of small commercial districts to provide for their daily needs. Namayo Avenue (97th Street), still an important route lined by a mercantile district, attracted entrepreneurs. The Hull Block, designed to house small retail businesses and apartments, was a successful example of this kind of commercial development within an urban neighbourhood.

The Hull Block is the only known building in Edmonton constructed

▲   148A

by William Roper Hull, a prominent Calgary civic leader and entrepreneur.

It was designed by architect E. C. Hopkins in the Edwardian Commercial style, quite common by 1914. Hopkins was generally considered "Edmonton's leading architect," and the "designer of some of the finest buildings in the Dominion of Canada," according to the Edmonton Bulletin. These included Regina City Hall, the Vancouver Opera House, and Calgary Normal School. Hopkins was appointed Alberta's first provincial architect in 1905 and went on to design some of the city's

most prominent landmarks, including the Marshall-Wells Building, the Great West Saddlery Company Building, the Horne and Pitfield Building, the Balmoral Block and the Prince of Wales Armouries.

Roy Gerolamy Residence

Constructed 1914
9823 91st Avenue
Designated Municipal Historic
Resource March 2000

The Roy Gerolamy Residence in the Mill Creek area is a pleasant example of the Arts and Crafts style featuring a square shape, asymmetrical massing, a bell-cast roof and a two-storey open veranda enclosed by triple square-cut columns. It is representative of the basic foursquare configuration. Foursquare homes were typically a two-storey box shape with four square rooms above three square rooms and a foyer. Foursquares were efficient to build, quite affordable and commonly offered by mail-order companies as pre-cut kit homes delivered to the nearest railway station. Most in Edmonton were simple in design, leaning more to a low-key Arts and Craft style.

The design of the Roy Gerolamy house expresses a solid appearance quite appropriate as a demonstration of the aspirations of the working class of the day.

Roy and Mary Gerolamy are thought to have built the house themselves. Roy was a carpenter.

Preserving more modest buildings such as theirs is a growing trend encouraged by Edmonton's historical preservation mandate.

ALL BUILT UP
A CENTURY OF GROWTH

One of our urban legends holds that an early booster was once asked to describe the size of Edmonton. He replied that it was as big as Chicago, "but it isn't all built up yet."

As the years have passed, Edmonton has grown in fits and starts, following the boom and bust cycles of the Alberta economy. Today the city is in many ways "all built up."

Edmonton began its real physical growth in 1870 when the first buildings were constructed in the Hudson's Bay Company Reserve located outside the palisades of Fort Edmonton. Squatters began to contend for the unsurveyed lots, leading to much resentment among the established settlers. A vigilance committee physically threw squatters' shacks over the riverbank into the valley below on several occasions.

In 1876 the Hudson's Bay Company (HBC) surveyed what today is the downtown, and three years later the first subdivision began when a single lot was sold. Anticipating that the Canadian Pacific Railway (CPR) would

◀ *Edmonton skyline in 2012.* 150A

take the northern transcontinental route through Edmonton, the HBC advertised lots in what it prematurely dubbed the City of Edmonton in 1881. When the CPR bypassed Edmonton in 1883, favouring instead the southern passes closer to the American border, the first speculative boom ended almost instantly. Nevertheless, real estate would remain the currency by which growth and wealth was measured for decades after these tentative beginnings.

The vast lands spreading from the First Meridian in Manitoba to the Rocky Mountains was laid out on a grid pattern adopted from the American township system. The Torrens system, in which the government retained the records of such surveys and allowed the disposition of patents and certificates of title at local land titles offices, facilitated the rapid transfer of ownership to individual, corporate

and homestead owners. Each township included 36 sections, each neatly adhering to this framework, with boundaries laid out north and south, east and west, on perpendicular lines, adjusted only by the regular correction lines to allow for longitudinal narrowing. The result was that roads, railways and urban development tended to fit the rectilinear pattern during the crucial years of first settlement and would not be challenged by urban designers until well into the twentieth century.

Land first became a commodity around Edmonton in 1882. The Hudson's Bay Company had owned the vast north-western territories until 1869 when it sold them to the new Dominion of Canada. Following the land transfer in 1870, the HBC retained substantial prime holdings, selling its first four hundred lots in 1882 and attracting great interest among settlers

and speculators across the new Dominion of Canada. McKay and Blake, the first real estate agency in Edmonton, announced their presence in the same year. In 1899 three individuals advertised themselves as real estate agents, although many others dealt in real estate more informally. Everyone considered himself a player in the booming real estate market that erupted around Edmonton, especially during the last decade before the Great War of 1914–18.

Fuelled by the Klondike gold rush, the community began to grow more rapidly. The arrival of the Canadian Northern Railway in Edmonton in 1902 added to the number of immigrants and settlers arriving in the district, as did the later Grand Trunk Pacific Railway.

Edmonton became a city in 1904, and Alberta a province in 1905, with Edmonton being declared its capital a year later. A true flood of eager settlers and business people

A century of growth has made a dramatic change to the city's skyline, seen between the two aerial shots taken in 1928 and 2011. 152A | 153A

arrived in the decade preceding the war. Between 1904 and the outbreak of the First World War, the city core was transformed from a city of wood to a city built of brick with a sense of permanence and a future.

The Edmonton Real Estate Exchange, established in 1909, represents the first concerted effort to regulate the rapid growth in land sales. In that year over 60 agencies and companies were listed in Edmonton and Strathcona, a number that would peak at 333 in 1914.

Between 1903 and 1914, 274 new subdivisions were laid out in the city. The HBC held its last big land sale in May 1912.

The Real Estate Exchange lasted only a short time, but it introduced the first local multiple listing service and laid the foundation for subsequent organization following the disruption of the First World War.

Demands for housing escalated during the pre-war boom years, and apartments became an important part of the Edmonton housing scene. The Arlington, completed in the fall of 1909, was the first apartment

building in Edmonton. For much of its life before it burnt down in 2005, the Arlington was home to Edmontonians prominent in the professions, business and society. Like other apartments at that time, such as LeMarchand Mansion (begun 1909, occupied 1911), the Algonquin (1915) and Westminster Apartments (1912), the Arlington offered its tenants modern conveniences, an appealing atmosphere and a central location near both the commercial urban centre and the legislature precinct.

Edmonton struggled to recover after the First World War, but by 1919 only about a hundred real estate agents remained in the city. It was not until 1927 that the Edmonton Real Estate Association was established, leading finally to the first legislation requiring the licensing of real estate sales people.

Between the world wars, many Edmonton subdivisions were cancelled. The building boom, fuelled by railway and real estate speculation, had left behind a vast urban area, only the core of which had been developed. Following the collapse of world markets in 1929, the Great Depression saw the sale of city land come almost to a complete halt. The city would remain the major landowner until after the Second World War.

By the time hostilities broke out again in Europe, Edmonton Real Estate Board membership had declined once more to a mere forty-six agents, reflecting the stagnation of Edmonton's growth and construction. Edmonton grew rapidly during the Second World War and was drawn further into the wider political and economic world. The wartime search for strategic reserves of oil soon would pay off, and the city would enter a new period of prosperity.

When oil was discovered near Leduc in 1947, a new generation of developers and speculators arrived in the city to help build the resurgent city. City population and personal income doubled between 1947 and 1957. Seven annexations allowed increased suburban growth to house the postwar baby boom between 1947 and 1960, allowing Edmonton, along with Calgary, to share the distinction of being the fastest-growing cities in Canada. Oil fuelled a dynamic period of growth from 1947 until 1981 that transformed the city. The city's landscape changed considerably, new subdivisions were built, modelled on automobile-oriented development, the more traditional grid layout being less favoured for curved streets and cul-de-sacs. Many of the newer neighbourhoods are less connected to each other in that they are surrounded by major roads with a few entry points into them. The older neighbourhoods' streets still open up to major arterial roads that run past them or through them, making them a little better connected in terms of walkability between districts. Shopping districts became car destinations with early strip-mall development later evolving into malls and most recently to big box stores.

The long period of economic growth ended suddenly with the 1982 recession. Up to this point new development and the modern era was seen as the way forward. Many of the city's significant buildings were lost to larger developments. The city's core character changed from being a vibrant pedestrian destination with many smaller buildings to one that was car-orientated with massive single buildings occupying entire blocks. Edmonton took on a more architecturally modest appearance. In reaction to the loss of many heritage structures, public pressure began to mount to ensure that City Hall establish some process to identify significant resources and try to save them.

From the mid-1990s the market had improved steadily; and by the first decade of the new century, Edmonton found itself in the middle of another upsurge in growth and prosperity. New subdivisions continue to be developed and the city's ring road, the Anthony Henday, is being filled in rapidly.

In 2008, a major international economic collapse brought a regional and local downturn, but Edmonton remains firmly of the opinion that, buffered by oil, it will continue to prevail.

▶ *Repurposing older buildings in the city has helped to transform and revitalize some of the older neighbourhoods, by bringing new uses to older attractive buildings.* 155A

THE HISTORICAL AND DISTINCT DISTRICTS OF EDMONTON

Neighbourhoods were the building blocks of urban growth in Edmonton, as they were in all western Canadian cities.

They rose and sometimes fell with the historical tides that swept the country and the province. Economic cycles and global wars were reflected in the fortunes of neighbourhoods and those who lived in them. Each boom period resulted in distinct neighbourhoods as developers and investors built new subdivisions to accommodate rising populations. The developments took on new architectural and urban forms as innovative styles, materials and transportation management practices influenced development forms. Driving through the city, one can easily see how the city expanded over the decades by identifying dominant architectural forms in each subdivision or neighbourhood.

◄ *The Dominion Hotel, listing a bit to one side and minus its distinctive tower, as it appeared in the Strathcona of 1969.* 156A

A flood could wash away decades of social life and business endeavour virtually overnight. Yet the neighbourhoods retained evidence of the forces that had shaped them. When the preservation movement emerged in Edmonton during the later 1960s and early 1970s, it frequently was at the neighbourhood level that the first sparks of resistance occurred, the river valley districts of Riverdale, Rossdale and Cloverdale a case in point.

It is in some of these historic neighbourhoods, including the downtown, that proactive planning policies and design guidelines were placed to capture the historical character of the areas ensuring that new development respected the links to the past. New streetscapes took their cues from the surrounding historical character and the period of predominant architectural style. The most significant example of this can be found on Edmonton's south side, in Strathcona.

OLD STRATHCONA PROVINCIAL HISTORIC AREA

In 1891, when the Calgary and Edmonton Railway reached the south banks of the North Saskatchewan River across from Edmonton, the community of South Edmonton sprang up almost overnight. Soon it had grown into the town of Strathcona (1899) and eventually the city of Strathcona (1907), becoming known as the "university city." The twin cities of Edmonton and Strathcona grew rapidly between 1891 and 1913, when amalgamation of the two cities into Greater Edmonton was realized, following a plebiscite the previous year. Over the following years "Old Strathcona"

survived, but declined as the push for urban growth was focused in other areas.

Old Strathcona was the earliest district to be seriously promoted as a neighbourhood worthy of preservation because of its historical value. In 1966, the Edmonton Historical Board, an advisory board to the Historical Development and Archives Branch, Parks and Recreation Department of the City of Edmonton, identified the group of buildings on Whyte Avenue between 103rd and 104th Streets as presenting a unique opportunity to preserve a turn-of-the-century commercial streetscape. The concept of "Strathcona Village," essentially a museum of turn-of-the-century buildings and commercial

activities, was developed at that time, and promotion was begun to obtain funds for the project. In 1969 the Historical Development and Archives Branch presented a report on Strathcona Village to City Council. Council referred the proposal to the South Edmonton Business Association and other interest groups, recommending that the federal government be asked to establish the area "as a National Historic Site" However, Ottawa did not consider the area significant enough to warrant such designation or funding.

In autumn of 1971, the Inner South Edmonton Charrette was sponsored by the City of Edmonton and the Department of Extension of the University of Alberta.

▲ *Strathcona's original boomtown architecture later became key to saving this historic district.* **158A**

Urban planners had brainstormed and created a plan, specifically the "Strathcona Village" and were now asking for public input. In the urban-planning context, a charrette was a good way to involve stakeholders beyond those normally interested in such issues, such as members of City boards and local business associations.

Some of the Charrette participants criticized the Strathcona Village proposal, on the grounds that it was confined primarily to one streetscape and therefore did not address the question of the destruction of the architectural heritage occurring throughout the area. Also, the concept of a turn-of-the-century museum was developed without consideration for its relationship to the neighbourhood, and many participants feared that if Strathcona Village were to encourage tourist trade, it would compound traffic problems without compensating the neighbourhood with improved services. In short, it would do little to improve the "quality of life" in Strathcona, a central goal of the Charrette.

Parties for and against the Village did share a common concern, however. The Charrette addressed the very real threat posed by a plan to build a major freeway through the old Strathcona Historical District. Participants agreed that if no action were taken on this front, most of the architectural heritage of Strathcona would be destroyed. As a consequence of this concern, some of the Charrette participants formed a group to pursue the broader questions of historical preservation and rejuvenation in Strathcona. Early in 1972, a breakthrough meeting took place in Strathcona consisting of the Public Affairs Committee of City Council, representatives of the Historical Board, members of the South Edmonton Business Association, members of the Charrette group and interested citizens. Discussed were possible approaches to the problem. At a second meeting, the Strathcona Historical Group was formed and, in July 1972, City Council approved a

study. A steering committee was appointed to prepare a proposal to develop plans and recommendations for the preservation and rejuvenation of Strathcona. The project, which began work in September 1972, was to take eight months.

Although its conceptual plan focused primarily on the civic-commercial core of Old Strathcona, the study area adopted by the historical group was the same as the boundaries of the Town of Strathcona as it was incorporated in 1899: University Avenue on the south, 109th Street on the west, the North Saskatchewan River on the north and Mill Creek on the east (97th Street was the actual town boundary). It contained most of the area which had been developed at the time of the 1912 amalgamation (excluding the University of Alberta and North Garneau), and therefore included much of the remaining architectural heritage of Strathcona. This larger area provided the opportunity to develop a program of rejuvenation and preservation within a neighbourhood context. Changing shopping habits and merchandising methods coupled with increasing traffic and parking problems had all contributed to the decline of the original retail area on Whyte Avenue. Proposed city transportation plans also had created much uncertainty about the future of the area. Public buildings had been scheduled for demolition, either

because they were obsolete for their original function or because they had to make way for proposed roadways. Some private buildings were deteriorating because their owners were either unable to demand rents sufficient to maintain their properties or unwilling to make the investment because of speculation about the future of the area. In combination, these factors contributed to a condition of decline in the core area.

While the core suffered from neglect and uncertainty, much of the residential area suffered from rapid change because of its proximity to the University and the city centre across the river, and also because of the age of many of its buildings. The residential area had been classified as "transitional," that is, subject to change to more intensive uses. Consistent with this planning concept, much of the area had been zoned for apartments, both walk-up and high-rise, which were replacing the original homes. These changes had been made at the expense of Strathcona's heritage.

Consistent with experiences in other communities at this time, the participants at the Inner South Edmonton Charrette demanded a greater voice in the planning of the future of their neighbourhood. The original sponsors of the Strathcona Historical Group took this position as a basic principle for planning for the rejuvenation and preservation of the cultural

heritage of Old Strathcona. The City Council decision to fund the Strathcona Historical Group's proposal was seen as consistent with this philosophy.

The Strathcona Historical Group first sprang into existence in the face of a threatened freeway project which would have run right through the middle of Old Strathcona, gutting the core of the historical district. The Group produced a report in 1973, which created the framework for the Old Strathcona Foundation. Much of the proposal changed over time, but this was

▲ *The restored Strathcona Fire Hall is now home to a theatre.* **160A**

the original mission for Old Strathcona.

Strathcona, The Asset of Heritage: A Plan for the Future, was a proposal prepared by the Strathcona Historical Group in June 1973. This report suggested that plans for the future of Strathcona should incorporate its historical resources, "which create the neighbourhood's identity, to provide a sense of continuity between the past, present and future." This was the

first real "mission statement" to emerge in the fight to preserve Old Strathcona. The Strathcona Historical Group recommended that the significance of Old Strathcona and its history be emphasized in its role as an important community neighbourhood. It also recommended that the Strathcona Historical Group project be viewed as the beginning of an alternative concept for Old Strathcona, that the recommended plan and program be complemented by an ongoing organizational capability, and that the City and the Strathcona Historical Group jointly explore the potential of designating selected buildings under the provisions of the Alberta Heritage Act. The final report, when presented to City Council in April 1974, had already garnered national support through Heritage Canada, which provided a million-dollar grant of support as a major pilot project, and cultural icons such as Pierre Berton who arrived in Edmonton to lobby City Council. City Council then approved the Old Strathcona Heritage Conservation Area, and Alberta promised support through the new Alberta Heritage Act. Such significant support resulted in the creation of the Old Strathcona Foundation (OSF) in 1974 to manage and account for these resources.

The area's distinctive architectural character set Strathcona aside and specific design guidelines and regulations were put into the local plan to regulate new infill and maintain

existing resources; these are specific to types of materials, building forms and scale of new development. Physical improvements were carried out to improve the streetscape; adding traditional lamp posts and street furniture as well as improvements to the pavement, to complement the turn-of-the-century buildings. Such initiatives ensure the fullest expression of one of Edmonton's foremost commercial and cultural districts.

Old Strathcona today is considered the flagship preservation district, and holds a special place in the hearts of Edmontonians.

Over the years the OSF, in co-operation with the City of Edmonton and with the support of the Old Strathcona Business Association, has worked to hold on to this special area. On January 29, 2007, the Old Strathcona Provincial Historic Area was established by Order in Council. This covered portions of the historical Strathcona, and ensured that it was now listed on the Alberta and Canadian registers of historic places. It includes the designated structures included in this book, and is only the second such area in Alberta, following that of Fort Macleod.

▲ *The Hub Cigar Store in April 1969, which has since burned down with the business moving east around the corner onto 103rd Street.* **161A**

Strathcona Public Library

Constructed 1913
8331 104th Street
Designated Municipal
Historic Site July 2004
Designated Provincial
Historic Resource July 1976
and February 2006

The Strathcona Public Library, built in a simplified Classical Revival style typical of public buildings in the Edwardian age, has stood at the centre of Strathcona as a cultural facility since its completion in 1913. For some years the Old Strathcona Foundation was located on the second floor and from that office emerged plans to preserve and interpret the story of Strathcona. This building is the oldest-surviving public library in Edmonton and one of the oldest in the province. Like the Strathcona Public Building on Whyte Avenue, it was completed in the year that amalgamation of Strathcona with Edmonton took place.

The Strathcona Public Library's distinctive façade is characterized by orange brick, a broad exterior entrance staircase, a classical door surround including engaged stone Ionic columns, a curved pediment, a stone lintel with the carved inscription "Public Library", sandstone detailing in the six-string courses and sill courses, wide cornices,

◄ 162A

sills and lintels, a fenestration pattern including an oculus window on the west, and a gable roof with stone parapets.

Classical elements were intended to give the building a sense of importance and dignity suitable to a place of learning located in the "university city" of Strathcona. The interior also included an auditorium and meeting rooms, and in 1948 the basement was converted to a children's library, enhancing its role as a centre for community life.

By the time of Strathcona's incorporation as a city in 1907, much of the rail and industrial activity had been attracted across the North Saskatchewan River to Edmonton following the coming of a transcontinental railway link to the capital. But Strathcona's civic pride burned brightly nonetheless. In 1910 the newly organized Strathcona Library Board began negotiations with the Carnegie Foundation for funds to construct a public library. The foundation was the means through which American industrialist and philanthropist Andrew Carnegie provided libraries to cities across North America, including the first public library in Edmonton. However, the Foundation's grant totalled only $15,000 for a small building constructed to a standardized plan.

The Strathcona Library Board believed that their new city's rapid growth required a larger library and turned down the Carnegie grant. Instead, the Strathcona Public Library would be funded by the newly amalgamated City of Edmonton.

In early 2006, the library underwent major renovations and expansion. Considerable effort was made to ensure the new addition would complement the original building and also be a positive asset to the adjoining McIntyre Park. The use of matching brick and window patterns links the two while ensuring the building still reads as one.

Gainer Block

Constructed 1902
10341 Whyte Avenue
Designated Provincial Historic
Resource April 1982

The Gainer Block, a two-storey rectangular commercial building with a restored red-brick façade, is situated on Whyte Avenue. The street-level display windows on either side of the recessed entrance, topped with small square-paned windows, served for elaborate displays at Christmas time as families bustled along Whyte Avenue looking for the perfect holiday game or fowl.

The Gainer Block represents the early development of Strathcona and provides evidence of the bustling young town's growth during the height of the pre-war commercial boom.

The Gainer Block was built by John Gainer (1858-1938), who played a prominent role in the development of the livestock-marketing industry in Western Canada. Gainer arrived in South Edmonton shortly after completion of the Calgary and Edmonton Railway, and started J. Gainer and Company, Butchers and Packers. By 1902 he would open his first single-storey frame shop on Whyte Avenue, soon to be replaced by the surviving structure. Gainer was one of the principal entrepreneurial

◀   164A

founders of his community and contributed personally to the expansion of Strathcona by donating land for parks, building roads and developing subdivisions. He gave employment to a significant part of the labour force in East Strathcona, as well as running his landmark shop.

The Gainer Block replaced the original wood frame butcher shop that had served Strathconians since 1893. The building served as office space as Gainer developed a more extensive slaughterhouse and meat packing-plant operation to the east of Strathcona on the Mill Creek Ravine.

The Gainer Block was the second brick building built on Whyte Avenue. In 1902 a Strathcona bylaw required brick construction to reduce the risk of fires that had proven so destructive in the predominatly wood constructed commerical cores of Western Canadian communities.

J. J. Duggan Residence
Constructed 1907
10515 Saskatchewan Drive
Designated Provincial Historic
Resource August 1982

John Joseph Duggan built this prominent brick residence in the year Strathcona was incorporated as a city. Nearby is the Duggan Bridge (1958), named for him, which replaced an earlier wooden bridge.

The Duggan House today provides offices for the Alberta Association of Architects, which restored it to its former glory after purchasing it from the City of Edmonton in 1982. This three-storey brick residence, with its high hipped roof and projecting gables, was considered a worthy home for the mayor of the new city. Duggan House was graced by an elegant front façade, with a veranda and balcony supported by Doric columns, which were later removed, but replaced by replicas when the structure underwent restoration. Its Ionic columns, with pronounced capitals, bespoke a desire for elegance and gracious living. This

▲ 167A

beautiful Queen Anne style dwelling also incorporated such accents as sandstone sills, quoins and keystones in its two distinctive round attic windows, designed to contrast with the predominant red brick.

John Duggan (1868-1952) was born near Fenelon Falls, Ontario, and moved to Alberta in 1891. He began the first lumberyard in Strathcona near 81st Avenue and 102nd Street, and operated this and other businesses until 1909 when he moved to a quarter section of land in south Edmonton, which eventually became the subdivision named Duggan in 1961. Duggan was elected to the first Strathcona Town Council in 1899 and later served as mayor in 1902 and 1903, and again during 1908–10. J. J. Duggan found himself embroiled in one of the many confrontations between Edmonton and Strathcona the year he became mayor. The "twin cities," located on opposite sides of the North Saskatchewan River, were rivals for the benefits of bridges, railways and other government largesse over the years. Sometimes, this competitive spirit spilled over into heated disagreements.

An Edmonton, Yukon and Pacific Railway (EY&P) construction gang arrived at a rail junction near the present 68th Avenue to install a switch connecting the Canadian Northern Railway's EY&P branch to the Canadian Pacific Railway's Calgary and Edmonton Railway main line shortly after the EY&P had completed its short line down Mill Creek and across the new bridge. The sometimes bitter legal wrangling between the CPR and Canadian Northern Railway came to a head when an EY&P crew tried to connect the lines. A crowd of agitated Strathconians gathered, while a CPR switch engine ran back and forth over the disputed tracks to prevent work on the planned switch. The CPR engine finally stopped on the spot where the switch was to be installed, leading to a tense few hours as they stood against a large crowd of Edmontonians who had arrived to reinforce Edmonton's interests. When it began to look as though the Strathcona interests would prevail, someone reminded the switch-engine crew they would have to move to permit the evening train from Calgary to pass. When the evening train pulled in, the EY&P gang and the Edmontonians immediately ripped up the CPR track so there would be room to install a switch to connect to their line – so quickly in fact the CPR switch engine could not get back out of the roundhouse.

The rail connection to Edmonton was the beginning of the end for Strathcona, which had been the end of steel for over a decade and the transportation cock of the walk. However, Duggan and some of his friends apparently cocked a snoot at Edmonton one night when they made the first furtive crossing of the bridge on a handcar before the Canadian Northern train could officially make it across on October 20, 1902!

W. H. Sheppard House
Constructed 1912
9945 86th Avenue
Designated Provincial Historic
Resource December 1981

The W. H. Sheppard house is an impressive example of the Georgian Revival style, featuring symmetrical massing, a steeply sloped hip roof crowned by a widow's walk, and wide wooden porches on the first and second floors of the north façade.

William Henry Sheppard was born in Ontario. After roaming the United States and Canada as a travelling building contractor, he arrived in Strathcona in 1894. He managed several hotels, including the Strathcona Hotel, which he purchased in 1896, and invested successfully in the local brewing industry. Despite the rigours of prohibition between 1916 and 1923, Sheppard prospered. Typical of the local entrepreneurial class, he soon entered local politics, serving terms as a town councillor for Strathcona in 1899, 1901, 1902, 1904, 1908 and 1909, and as mayor in 1906. In 1907 he constructed the impressive Sheppard Block on Whyte Avenue. He played a leading role in the amalgamation debates that led to the merging of the twin cities of Strathcona and Edmonton.

168A.. ▶

Douglas Block

Constructed 1912
10442 Whyte Avenue
Designated Provincial Historic
Resource January 1982

This three-storey commercial block located on the north side of Whyte Avenue in the heart of historic Strathcona district has a locally manufactured red-brick façade accentuated by classical details such as stone pilasters, keystones above its windows, and a central pediment with decorative detailing.

In 1899, the year the settlement of South Edmonton was incorporated as the town of Strathcona, James and Robert Douglas established a small general goods store in the community.

By 1911 it had grown into the largest general retail establishment in Strathcona with sixteen staff members. The Douglas brothers became real estate speculators, typical of businessmen of the day.

The following year, when the City of Strathcona amalgamated with Edmonton, they commissioned well-known Strathcona architects Wilson and Herrald to design a new commercial building on Whyte Avenue.

The Douglas Block was constructed in 1912 during the final years of Edmonton's pre-war building boom.

James Douglas served as the president of the Strathcona Board of Trade, the member of Parliament for Strathcona and the mayor of Edmonton.

169A ▶

Connaught (Strathcona) Armouries

Constructed 1912
10310 85 Avenue
Designated Provincial Historic
Resource February 1979
Designated Municipal Historic
Resource March 2007

The Connaught Armouries, located at the intersection of 85th Avenue and 103rd Street, was named for H.R.H. Prince Arthur William Patrick Albert, Duke of Connaught (1850-1942), the favoured son of Queen Victoria and the Governor General of Canada from 1911 to 1916. The Connaught is the oldest remaining armoury of this style in Alberta.

The Brown Construction Company of Winnipeg placed the successful bid and began building in 1911. The Connaught remained a central part of Strathcona military and social life for decades. Like other armouries of the time, it included a rifle range and shooting gallery, as well as what the Edmonton Bulletin called "one of the best and truest bowling floors in the city" in its basement. It also included the usual parade hall, reading room, regimental offices and mess hall.

The Connaught Armouries is a distinctive two-storey structure of orange brick, characterized by a sandstone trim typical of the larger public buildings in Strathcona before the First World War. An arched entrance is topped with decorative and symbolic sandstone "cannon balls" similar to other period armouries like the Prince of Wales in Edmonton's Central MacDougall neighbourhood. A pronounced parapet surmounts the façade, while subdued fortress-like dentilations over the entrance enhance the military aspect of the building.

Strathcona had a military presence as early as 1905 when veterans of the South African War petitioned for the creation of a mobile militia unit in their town. In 1908 the Alberta Mounted Rifles was established (renamed the 19th Alberta Dragoons a year later). The Dragoons petitioned Militia Minister Sam Hughes for their own armoury. When they succeeded, the news was greeted with much enthusiasm by the Strathcona Plaindealer, which reported the arrival of the plans at the new CPR station on May 9, 1911. The Dragoons were the first unit mobilized during the First World War and saw extensive service, fighting at such well-known engagements as Ypres, the Somme and Vimy Ridge. In 1936 the 19th Alberta Dragoons absorbed the Alberta Mounted Rifles Regiment and A Company, 13th Machine Gun Battalion and, in 1946, the Edmonton Fusiliers as well. The continued presence of the Connaught Armoury at this conspicuous location provides an important reminder of the military's long-time presence in Edmonton and its effect on the development of the city. Over the years, hundreds of Strathconians who trained at the Connaught served overseas in numerous battles. The Regimental Colours now are located in Holy Trinity Anglican Church.

171A ▶

Bard Residence and Carriage House

Constructed 1912
10544 84th Avenue
Designated Municipal Historic
Resource June 1998
Designated Provincial Historic
Resource June 2000

The Delmar Bard Residence and its carriage house constitute an impressive foursquare house faced in stretcher-bond red brick with a square one-storey flat-roofed addition and a detached two-storey carriage house.

Extolled as one of the city's finest homes in the local press, the Bard Residence was built in 1912 on a newly acquired lot in Strathcona. The Bard residence was quite highly crafted, and its appearance signalled that the Strathcona of the early 1900s could boast an established upper middle class. The construction cost – $6,500 – was a substantial sum at the time.

Bard emigrated from St. Paul, Minnesota, in 1896 and began his career in 1907 as an Indian Agent and a road inspector for the provincial government in the new City of Strathcona. His shrewd business and real estate investments allowed him to live in a grand style beyond the means of his public-servant colleagues. He owned a butcher shop on Whyte Avenue, and he invested his combined government and business incomes in various successful real estate ventures.

▲   172A

This notable residence, designed by Keith Brothers, is an upscale model of the foursquare design with the simple, symmetrical qualities considered appropriate for a respectable yet comfortable residence of the Edwardian period. Constructed of brick with stone details, a decorative frieze and a full-length porch surmounted by a balcony, the house was topped by a pyramidal roof and bracketed bell-cast eaves. Designed in the Georgian Revival style, a popular classical revival form of the period, the house exhibits several features that distinguish it from Strathcona's other large brick homes. A spacious flat-roofed conservatory with large windows intended to catch the eastern sun was attached to the residence soon after construction. A

large carriage house with second-floor living quarters (now converted to a garage) is situated at the back of the lot, a rare surviving example of such a building in an urban centre. Bard installed a turntable in his driveway similar to those in railway roundhouses that rotated vehicles 180 degrees and eliminated the worry of backing onto the busy street. The home had many noteworthy modern conveniences, including a central vacuum-cleaning system.

One of the grander residences of Old Strathcona, the Delmar Bard Residence is a prominent local landmark. After Bard's death in 1938, his widow continued to reside in the house until her passing in 1955.

ROSSDALE

Ross Flats, later known as Rossdale, remains one of the oldest and most historically significant districts in Edmonton. However, it was not until more recent times that its importance to the history of Edmonton was fully embraced by the city. Rossdale is bounded by the sharp curve of the broad North Saskatchewan River to the south, and extends northward to 97th Avenue, Bellamy Hill, 99th Avenue and MacDonald Drive, and westward to 106th Street. Within this small area the first agricultural fairs were held, the new Province of Alberta proclaimed by Prime Minister Wilfrid Laurier, two of the five Fort Edmontons were built and a fur era burial ground was

located. The latter languished for decades under a roadway, but has since been rediscovered and freed of pavement. The flats weathered the ravages of repeated floods, and for over a century became the site of power generation for a growing city.

The district's namesake, Donald Ross (1840–1915), spent nine years prospecting for gold in California before arriving in the Edmonton settlement in the early 1870s, hoping to homestead on the flats below the Methodist mission established by Reverend John McDougall. In 1876 Ross established the Edmonton Hotel, the city's first hotel, on these flats. In 1881 he began

View of Rossdale and Rossdale Road from the Hotel MacDonald.
173A

to mine coal on his lot. Ross Flats became one of the first industrial sites in the city with a brewery, icehouse and lumberyard.

In 1891 the Edmonton Electric Light Company built its first power plant here, the first example of public land use. In 1897 Dowler's Mill was opened, initiating the industrial use of the flats. As residential development progressed during the pre-First World War commercial boom, Donald Ross School was built in 1912 to accommodate the needs of the

burgeoning population. By June 1915, when a devastating flood swept through the neighbourhood, destroying many of the industrial and residential structures, Rossdale was a vital working-class area with some middle-class management, business people and students living there as well.

The city reversed its policy of converting land in Rossdale into parkland after decades of slow decline, recognizing that it was and is a community. The local plan identified public improvements as one of the best ways to revitalize Rossdale. As

a major land holder, the city developed specific design guidelines for a new residential development to preserve and enhance the historic character of Rossdale. The city sold off parcels of land; it then held design competitions to ensure the best schemes were developed. The area benefitted from a new design plan and streetscape, and interpretive elements were installed throughout to distinguish the Rossdale neighbourhood.

In recent years Rossdale has been at the epicentre of a public debate about

▲ *1904 Rossdale Brewery Building.*
174A

the future development of the power plant and its impact on the burial grounds and archaeological sites that truly represent the kernel from which the city grew. Rossdale also remains the location of other historic commercial and institutional buildings such as the Ortona Armoury and the old Rossdale Brewery.

Children's Shelter

Constructed 1911
9540 101st Street
Designated Municipal Historic
Resource March 2001

The Edmonton Children's Shelter, a home for neglected and delinquent children, professed to be the best of its kind in Canada. Designed with a Classical Revival influence, the building is a well-known three-storey, flat-roof structure. The symmetrical massing, projecting central raised entry and north-south interconnected balconies form the principle features of the building. Its rich detailing consists of orange-red-brick cladding, an arched doorway canopy with bracketing, keystone voussoirs surmounting the windows, decorative pilasters flanking the entrance, and a decorative roof frieze with entablature. The roof is encircled by a tin cornice and tin-capped parapet.

In 1911 the city began construction of a new children's shelter on Edmonton's first exhibition grounds on land it had acquired from the Hudson's Bay Company. The new shelter replaced the small existing shelter at 47 Cameron Street in Edmonton's east end. An addition was built in 1914.

The new shelter served as a home for needy children until its closure in 1925, when it was turned over to the Salvation Army, which operated it as Grace Hospital

▲ 175A

until 1942. From 1942 until 1944, the building was used by American servicemen constructing the Alaska Highway and was known as the Little America Transit Hotel. Wartime use ended by 1944 and it changed once again, becoming the twelve-suite Ross Flats Apartments.

James Henderson (1861–1932), a leading Edmonton architect, designed the 1911 Children's Shelter. Originally from England, Henderson established his practice in Edmonton some time before 1907. He was elected a Fellow of the Royal Institute of British Architects and joined the Alberta Association of Architects the same year, serving as president of the association in 1914. Henderson designed many residential buildings in Edmonton, including the

Glenora mansion of Charles Cross, the provincial attorney general, in 1912. He also designed a number of notable commercial and civic buildings, including the Brown Block (1911), later known as the Brighton Block, and Fire Hall No. 5 (1910).

Apart from the demolition of the 1914 addition and some alterations to the north and south balconies, and to the openings on the rear elevation, the original exterior character of this building is intact.

Hudson's Bay Company Stables (Ortona Armouries)

Constructed circa 1914
9722 102nd Street
Designated Municipal Historic Resource August 2004

Now better known as the Ortona Armouries, this structure in Rossdale was first built by the Hudson's Bay Company as a stable. Its original brick exteriors remain intact, as does some architectural detailing, though much of the detailing of the original building was covered in subsequent renovations, especially when the stable was taken over as the Ortona Armouries.

The old hoist penthouse, covered in pressed-metal siding, can be seen on the southern rooftop. Also visible in the brick-and-sandstone parapet are eight brick pilasters dividing the east façade into seven asymmetrical bays, a brick dentil course surmounting the sandstone lintels on the upper-floor windows, and prominent carved-sandstone cartouches and the Hudson's Bay Company coat of arms above the main entrance.

Decorative floor elements in terrazzo and tile, including naval symbols with their historical associations, remain from the time when the Ortona Armouries housed H.M.C.S. Nonsuch. A fireplace remains in the naval mess hall.

176A ▶

Rossdale Power Plant

10155 96th Avenue
Designated Provincial Historic
Resource October 2001

The current Rossdale Power Plant, located on the north bank of the North Saskatchewan River, was constructed during the middle part of the twentieth century. It is the only historic power plant of this scale remaining in Alberta. The Rossdale Power Plant's historical designation applies to three separate but interrelated structures: the Low Pressure Plant, including the Turbine House and Boiler House, Pumphouse No. 1, and the Administration Building.

▲ 177A

The three buildings, constructed between 1931 and 1954, represent the history of electrical-power generation in Edmonton and in Alberta.

The site is associated with Maxwell Dewar, a prominent architect responsible for designing part of the plant who later served as Edmonton's city architect. As a municipally run electrical utility, the plant illustrates government involvement in industrial enterprise. Finally, the three historic elements of the Rossdale Power Plant are good examples of architectural design, style and construction methods characteristic of the late 1920s and 1930s. Its functional design was influenced by contemporary industrial and factory architecture in the United States.

Construction of the first powerhouse began in July 1902. A water-intake, powerhouse and sedimentation basin were built on the site, and the first water mains and sewers were constructed. In 1903 the town built a home for the engineer in charge of the powerhouse just north of the power plant and east of 104th Street. The same year a fence around the powerhouse property was constructed. In 1908 a spur line from the Edmonton, Yukon and Pacific Railway was run down to the powerhouse. Building occurred between 1907 and 1913 and again in the 1920s. In 1930 City Council approved a new five-year plan of expansion for the Rossdale Power Plant that involved the removal of part of the old plant and the construction of a new one, including a coal conveyor that extended westward.

Further construction occurred on the west side of the power plant in 1938 and again in 1954.

Electricity has been generated continuously on the site since 1903. The plant is one of the oldest-surviving examples of mid-twentieth century industrial design in Alberta; no other steel-and-brick buildings of this size and period remain in Edmonton. The Low Pressure Plant is also notable in that its expansion maintained Dewar's original style, with six additions over a twenty-two-year period, as the site evolved to incorporate technological advances.

Parkview Apartments and Foote House

Constructed 1914
10612 97th Avenue
Designated Municipal Historic
Resource July 2002
Richard Foote House
Constructed 1907
9704 106th Street
Designated Municipal Historic
Resource July 2002

Both these red-brick buildings, located near the dome of the Legislature Building, were constructed for Richard E. Foote. Richard Foote and his partner Nathaniel W. Purcell were general contractors whose office in the Tegler Building was responsible for many remarkable pre-war structures. Purcell and Foote appear to have constructed both buildings.

▲ 178A

The front façade of the Parkview Apartments, facing 97th Avenue, shows the original 1914 brick detail and stone trims, including banded rusticated brickwork, doorway voussoirs and keystone, and the three arched windows' brick dressing and keystones. The effect is enhanced by stone window sills and lintels, three recessed panels between the first and second floor windows, the continous stone lintel at the lower first-floor window level, and a stone cornice capping the rusticated brickwork. The decorative metal cornice and small brick parapet are of interest, as are the timber sash

windows, including arched fanlight windows with three panes and a half-circle pane. The roof is characterized by brick chimney stacks and pressed-metal penthouses.

The east façade of the Foote residence, fronting on 106th Street, shows the original 1907 materials, including brick detail and stone trims. Banded rusticated brickworks, corbelled brick columns around the gable window, and a stone belt-course are incorporated. The front porch is on this side, with square fluted

columns on brick and stone piers, a central portico with a circular patterned relief, and brick dentilation featured in the eaves. A brick bay window stretches from the ground level to the upper storey, which is surmounted by a gable. Similar detail in stone, brick, and woodwork make all the façades of this building visually appealing.

The roof of this two-storey house includes details of the original metal sheeting, while the pitch of the bell-cast hip roof is low, with overhanging eaves. There are bell-cast

▲ 179A

hip dormers in three of the façades, and the chimney features a corbelled brick cap.

Richard Foote arrived in Edmonton in 1903 to work in the construction business. When he died in 1948 he was remembered for one of his first projects, the Alberta Hotel on Jasper Avenue. Other projects singled out in the Edmonton Bulletin at that time included the Civic Block, St. Mary's Children's Home (1923), and Athabasca Hall. Foote also helped build the Ponoka Mental Institute.

In 1908 Foote was living in the house which preceded the Parkview on these lots, but by 1909 Dr. Daniel Revell was the occupant. Revell was probably the most notable occupant of Foote house, given that he was the first provincial bacteriologist, who had "a distinguished career as a teacher, physician, analyst, surgeon, professor, pathologist, criminologist, hand-writing expert, research scientist and author." Foote was elected to City Council during 1934, 1935 and 1936. He served on the Finance Committee in 1935 and 1936, and was

the Edmonton Exhibition Association representative in 1936. Foote also ran unsuccessfully for mayor, being defeated in November 1936 when Mayor Joseph Clarke was re-elected. During 1944 he became an assistant building inspector with the City Planning Department, with offices then at the McLean Block.

◄ *1960s aerial view of McCauley.*
180A

targeted for infrastructure improvements to mitigate some consequences of the large concentration of social agencies in the area. Traffic calming measures were also required, resulting in a quieter, well-landscaped street (see St. Josaphat Ukrainian Catholic Cathedral for more details).

The Boyle area faced decades of decline as the city's growth moved west of 97th Street. Various revitalization initiatives have been undertaken; Old Town Market, the Downtown Development Corporation's Main Street Program, and more recently the Quarters Project. The heritage buildings represent some of the oldest commercial stock in the city and the local plan's specific design regulations ensure that resources are kept and new development is sympathetic. The Quarters urban design plan and development project identifies pedestrian corridors, heritage blocks, new park space and links to the surrounding streets.

Plans to re-establish some of the former "respectability" of the neighbourhood have proven difficult to achieve at times, but the new plans and the important heritage represented by the buildings located along its streets hold out hope for the future.

BOYLE–MCCAULEY

McCauley lies between Norwood Boulevard and 105th Avenue, and between the LRT tracks angling to the northeast and 101st Street. McCauley was named for Matt McCauley, first mayor of the Town of Edmonton and a key figure in the early history of Edmonton. Boyle Street, formerly 103A Avenue, running through McCauley, was one of the first true Edmonton neighbourhoods and the Boyle district is home to the city's original commercial neighbourhood. It most likely was named for J. R. Boyle, who built the Lambton Block. Boyle-McCauley

had become a byword for rundown and distressed inner-city neighbourhoods in Edmonton. But significant investment into the neighbourhoods, official recognition of its unique character, and efforts to retain and promote many of the citys oldest resources is contributing to the areas revitalization as a vibrant district again. Boyle was primarily commercial, while McCauley was residential, and this is reflected in the building stock that remains. McCauley is also home to "Church Street" (96th Street), noted for one of the largest concentrations of churches on a single street in Canada. The street was

▲ 181A ▲ 181B

St. Josaphat Ukrainian Catholic Cathedral

Constructed 1939
10825 97th Street
Designated provincial historic
resource August 1983

St. Josaphat Ukrainian Catholic
Cathedral is a large Byzantine style
church closely associated with the history
of Ukrainian Catholic life in Alberta.
It is an outstanding representation of
Ukrainian-Canadian church architecture.

The cathedral is distinguished by its seven
domes. The large central dome is open to the
interior and is flanked by six smaller, closed
domes. Based on the nine-part cruciform
plan with the apse oriented to the east, a
characteristic of the largest Ukrainian
Baroque designs, St. Josaphat exhibits a
polychromatic red-brick exterior veneer
embellished with darker brick pilasters

and inlaid cream-coloured crosses, and
highlighted by dark-brick pilasters and
seven striking cupolas that represent the
sacraments and the gifts of the Holy Spirit.
Beyond the columned entry portico, the
entrance presents a long, wide staircase
and portico extending the full width of
the façade with eight Tuscan columns.
The painted iconostasis, wall frescoes and
the black marble wall with stained-glass
windows are also notable features. The iconic
paintings of Professor Julian Bucmaniuk
have decorated the cathedral interior since
the 1950s. He often used parishioners as
his models for holy men and women.

The building's highly regarded architect,
Philip Ruh, was an Oblate priest sent to
work as a missionary among Canada's
Ukrainian Catholics. Having educated
himself in the aesthetics and spiritual
sensibilities of Ukrainian Catholics, he

designed over thirty such churches
throughout Western Canada and Ontario.
St. Josaphat is the most extravagant example
of Ruh's work in Alberta. It speaks of a
strong sense of historical continuity with
the early Byzantine traditions of the
church. It also reflects Ruh's appreciation
for Ukrainian Baroque values.

Ukrainian Catholics on the Canadian
Prairies found themselves largely lacking
clergy familiar with their language,
culture and liturgy until the Ukrainian
Basilian Fathers arrived in Edmonton
in 1902. The Basilians built the original
St. Josaphat Church in 1904 under the
leadership of Reverend Sozont Dydyk.

In 1938, plans were prepared
for a larger building that could
accommodate the church's growing
number of parishioners, as well as

commemorate the 950th anniversary of the Christianization of the Ukraine.

Construction on the church began in 1939 but was not completed until the mid-1940s. It was dedicated in 1947, and the following year a papal bull divided the Ukrainian Catholic Exarchate of Winnipeg, which included all of Canada, into three administrative districts located in Edmonton, Winnipeg and Toronto. As the only Ukrainian Catholic church in Edmonton, St. Josaphat was designated a cathedral with Most Reverend Neil N. Savaryn appointed Bishop Ordinary for the Apostolic Exarchate of Edmonton, serving Alberta and British Columbia.

St. Josaphat Ukrainian Catholic Cathedral anchors an entire block of religious institutions to the west of Church Street, a portion of 96th Street that a persistent urban myth alleges that *Ripley's Believe It Or Not* declared "the largest concentration of churches in the world." In addition to St. Josaphat on this city block are Mary Queen of the Martyrs, a Vietnamese Catholic church, formerly Immaculate Conception Roman Catholic Church, the oldest house of worship on the street (1906), and Sacred Heart Church of the First Peoples, formerly Sacred Heart Roman Catholic Parish (1913) and its attendant school and learning centres.

As well, 96th Street features an outstanding collection of ecclesiastical architecture running the gamut from the Byzantine and French Gothic Revival to the modern, including St. Barbara's Russian Orthodox Cathedral; the Chinese United Church, previously called Central United Church, (1953); the Mustard Seed Street Church, formerly Central Baptist Church (1912); St. John's Lutheran Church (1971); Ansgar Lutheran Church (1939); First Christian Reformed Church (1948); St. Peter's Lutheran Church (1928); and Mui Kwok Buddhist Temple, formerly Church of Christ Disciples (circa 1914); and the Ukrainian Greek Catholic Association, the former Cornerstone Church of God (1917). St. Stephen's the Martyr Anglican Church (1914) still stands, though it is no longer used as a place of worship. An architectural firm now operates in this space and is credited with saving an endangered historical treasure from almost certain demolition.

◀ 182A

▲ 183A

Rehwinkel Parsonage

Constructed 1913
9608 110th Avenue
Designated Municipal Historic
Resource June 2004

The Rehwinkel Parsonage is a modest Victorian gable-fronted, homestead-style house with a porch on the south elevation that originally wrapped around the east elevation as well. Gables are found on the front and rear, which also has a lean-to addition.

The front elevation's principal features are the porch, the decorative shingle detailing in the apex of the gable, and a modest frieze surround. The gable is framed by returned eaves, adding to the picturesque impression. The remainder of the face has timber lap-siding. The east porch was removed to accommodate the extension at the rear of St. Peter's Lutheran Church.

The Rev. Alfred M. Rehwinkel was the founder of Concordia College in Edmonton.

He was born in Wisconsin and ordained in the Lutheran Church in 1910 before serving as a missionary in Western Canada until 1914. He then became pastor of St. Peter's Lutheran Church and taught at Concordia College from 1921 to 1928.

John McNeill Residence

Constructed circa 1907
11217 97th Street
Designated Municipal Historic
Resource February 2005

This Victorian dwelling exhibits some Queen Anne characteristics, an uncommon style in Edmonton, though common in Ontario. An attractive two-storey, hipped-roof house with lower cross gables, the McNeill residence is clad with buff and orange brick and stone masonry. On all façades the buff brick is framed with orange brick detailing, including the edges of the quoins and the cogging details at the eave and gable levels. There also is a brick banding-belt course above the stone foundation. Many features are rare in Edmonton, especially the fieldstone foundation, the widow's walk on the roof, which is no longer present, and the two-toned angled brick atop the exterior brickwork. Also notable is the decorative relief brick at the bottoms of some windows and the decorative woodcarvings on the soffits.

The front façade is characterized by its gabled peak extension with returned eaves. A decorative frieze of rosettes linked by disks circles the house at the eave. An arched window in the gable has decorative voussoirs with a rough brick hood mould surrounding them.

John McNeill was born in Scotland in 1871. In 1910 he immigrated to Alberta hoping to farm, but soon moved to Edmonton, where he bought Twin City Transfer. He soon built the company into one of the largest moving businesses in Alberta, becoming the sole baggage agent for the Canadian Pacific Railway, as well as developing interests in taxi, bus, transfer, cartage and storage businesses. McNeill launched

▲ *The McNeill house in 1913.* 184A

Edmonton's first taxi service, and at one time also owned all its ambulances. He built Edmonton's first aircraft hangar at what later would become Blatchford Field, the first municipal "air harbour" in Canada.

Lambton Block

Constructed circa 1914
11045 97th Street
Designated Municipal Historic
Resource September 2003

The Lambton Block is eccentrically shaped with six sides, conforming to the irregular shape of its lot. The principal façades face 97th Street and 110A Avenue with a prominent corner façade addressing the streets. The original brick pilasters at the ground floor frame the commercial window, now bricked-in, while a sign band and cornice wrap around the principal façades. The building is constructed of reinforced concrete with red tapestry brick and is clad in Tyndall stone. The reinforced, cast-in-place concrete structural system was considered bold and innovative at the time and was designed to be fireproof. The building originally had commercial retail spaces on the ground floor, but these were later converted to apartment suites.

The Lambton Block was built for John Robert Boyle, a prominent and influential politician during Alberta's early years. Boyle was born in Sykeston, Ontario, in 1871. At the age of fourteen, he lost his father and took responsibility for a family of nine. He continued his education on his own initiative and began teaching in Lambton County before moving west to Regina in 1894 and to Edmonton in 1896. While teaching, he also studied law and in 1899 was admitted to the bar and began a distinguished legal career. Boyle was named a King's Council in 1912 and Judge of the Supreme Court of Alberta in 1924.

Boyle's political career began with campaigning for Frank Oliver and involvement with the Liberal Party. In 1904 Boyle was elected to Edmonton's first City Council as an alderman, and in 1905 he was elected to Alberta's first Legislature. He served as minister of Education, attorney general, and leader of the Opposition. Alberta's first summer village was named after Boyle's summer cottage, Kapasiwin, located on Lake Wabamum, where the powerful and influential gathered to plan political campaigns and legislation. The cottage still stands.

By 1912 Boyle was sufficiently successful to enable him to contract Roland Lines to build the Lambton Block, named for his native Lambton County in Ontario.

▶ *J. R. Boyle, third from the right, attends the Edmonton Police parade in 1923 against the backdrop of the old Civic Block. Emily Murphy and Police Chief Anthony Shute flank him on the left, while the tall man to the right is Cloverdale's Pete Anderson, whose bricks were used in many Edmonton buildings.* 185B

104TH STREET
(WAREHOUSE DISTRICT)

The downtown warehouse district's 104th Street contains the last and largest collection of turn of the century brick warehouses in Edmonton. Industrial architecture from this time period is relatively rare in Edmonton, making this street an obvious choice for infrastructure investment and revitalization.

The street developed as a result of the economic boom shortly after the turn of the century in Edmonton and northern Alberta. The nearby railway yards located to the north of 104th Avenue and spur lines running south down the lanes between the adjacent streets, especially on 104th Street, meant suppliers quickly established their business and distribution centres in this neighbourhood to ensure easier access to the larger markets resulting from the urban growth and expansion of settlement in the surrounding districts.

With the warehouses disappearing over time, the Downtown Plan recognized their value and the need to take positive action. New streetscaping, reflective of the surrounding building stock and time period, was developed and parallel initiatives to restore and convert the heritage warehouses transformed the street into a vibrant pedestrian street. In the summer, automobile traffic on the two blocks closest to Jasper Avenue is blocked off for a much-attended open-air farmers market. Also successful is the Jasper entrance to this reborn street following the 2008 replacement of the Hotel Cecil that carefully mirrors the Birks building across the way while making an early 21st century statement. It is pleasantly ironic that development pressure in the area led to stricter design regulations, ensuring

▲ *Early photograph of 104 Street, north of Jasper Avenue.* **186A**

that new development takes on the heritage character that makes the district unique.

Canadian Consolidated Rubber Company Building
Constructed 1913
10249 104th Street
Designated Municipal Historic
Resource November 2001

Edmonton's Warehouse District was at the commercial heart of the city during its formative decades when Revillon Frères and the Hudson's Bay Company supplied the advancing northern resource frontier. The district bustled noisily day and night with trains, horse teams and trucks transferring goods from the railway spurs that interpenetrated the many warehouses.

The Canadian Consolidated Rubber Company warehouse is a strong reminder of the importance of the district in Edmonton's history. Designed in an early commercial style, it was originally planned for retail use on the first floor, while the upper floors housed distribution and warehouse storage space. One of the remaining prominent warehouses along 104th Street, the building adds an important visual element to the streetscape.

This attractive commercial block was designed and built by the Canadian Stewart Company of Toronto. In 1911 the Montreal-based Canadian Consolidated Rubber Company branched into Edmonton, becoming the prime tenant in the Ker

◀ 187A

Building on 102nd Avenue and 104th Street. The Ker block was destroyed by fire in 1913, one of the worst in early Edmonton, resulting in the deaths of two people as well as the destruction of several buildings. William Allen, owner of the building from 1913 to 1935, was in charge of the Winnipeg investment consortium that purchased this site and constructed a new building for the Canadian Consolidated Rubber Company. The warehouse is a rectangular red-brick, five-and-one-half-storey building with five bays, possessing a more vertical emphasis than adjacent warehouses in the Warehouse District. Verticality is achieved by having the centre bay of windows located at the stair landing rather than on each floor. The building relates well to its immediate neighbours, the Horne and Pitfield Building to the north and the Revillon Building to the south. Notable elements include the brick-corbelled cornice, the two-storey entrance feature, the simulated quoin treatment of brick, and the bracketed shelf over the door and stair-landing window. The building also has a prominent date stone at the top that reads 1913.

Exposed portions of the east, north and south walls of the building were used extensively for painted advertising by various tenants. Faint reminders of the colourful lettering typical of advertisements of the time extol Dominion Rubber Systems Alta

and Clark Bro. Co. Ltd., Paper Stationers. Other surviving examples of painted signage in Edmonton include those on the Gibson Block and the H. V. Shaw Building.

◀ 188A

Armstrong Block

Constructed 1912
10125 104th Street
Designated Municipal Historic
Resource June 2001
Designated Provincial Historic
Resource September 2003

The elegant Armstrong Block recalls
the optimism of the Edmonton
business community at the height of
the pre-First World War economic
boom. It is further illustrative of the
diversification of warehouse, office
and residential accommodation in
the developing Warehouse District at
the turn of the twentieth century.

The strong visual form and massing of the
Armstrong Block gave it an important
presence on 104th Street that effectively
anchored the southern edge of the 104th
Street Warehouse District prior to the
construction of the Birks Building in
1929. Along with the nearby Great
West Saddlery Building, it is one of the
most southerly warehouse, office and
apartment structures of the remaining
104th Street group of buildings.

Architect David Hardy designed this
mixed-use building that originally housed
a wholesale business on the first floor
and single-room offices and apartments
on the upper floors. The ordering of the

189A ▶

▲ 190A

floors, as articulated by stone banding and punched window penetrations, gives the building a clear definition of its scale. The front elevation is clad with a pressed red brick common to other buildings in the Warehouse District. The side and rear elevations are clad with a red utility brick. Decorative stone on the main entrance, unusual decorative parapet capping with corner crenelations, contrasting windowsills and brick pilasters give the building a strong presence.

Highlights include the entablature with its inscription and decorative carving, and the main entrance voussoir with keystone and a flat transom with a single light.

Hardy originally trained as an engineer and was eventually registered as a member of the Alberta Association of Architects in December 1920. He entered into an architectural partnership with John Martland shortly after designing the Armstrong Block. The building contractor was Reed, McDonald, Brewster Ltd.

The Armstrong Block has had only minor alterations over its history and remains an integral part of the Warehouse District's

▲ *Warehouses on 104th Street in 1914 include the Armstrong Block, foreground, and the Great West Saddlery, Kelly and McKenny buildings. The Revillon Block is in the background.* 190B

streetscape and character. It continues to play a key role in the preservation of the remaining warehouses in the district.

HIGHLANDS

The Highlands neighbourhood today lies between Ada Boulevard and 118th Avenue, and between 50th Street and 67th Street. Originally known as the Lower Settlement, it was occupied by three Hudson's Bay Company employees. In 1888 John A. McDougall purchased the property, but by 1910, Magrath, Holgate and Company, acting as brokers for the McDougall interests, were promoting the area for residential development. A contest resulted in the name Highlands.

To promote the neighbourhood as one with a certain cachet, construction was limited to homes valued over a certain amount. The Magrath Mansion and the Holgate Residence both were built in the Highlands on Ada Boulevard.

Today the Highlands Historical Society exercises its vigilance in preserving and promoting this area, and its large collection of period homes by working closely with the City of Edmonton.

▲ *Mother and children walking on boardwalk in front of new houses in Highlands.* **191A**

▶ *Magrath Mansion completed in 1913, by one of Highlands' developers to set the tone for new development is now one of Highlands most iconic buildings.* **191B**

Eda Owen Residence

Constructed 1912
11227 63rd Street
Designated Provincial Historic
Resource March 1994

The First World War encouraged
or compelled many women to take
an active role in the workplace.
Eda Owen, Edmonton's "weather
lady," was one such woman.

Eda Owen, Canada's first female weather
observer, lived in this modest wood frame
foursquare house built by lumberman
Garnett M. Meiklejohn. Eda came to
Edmonton in 1908 with her husband
Herbert, a retired sea captain. When he
became a weatherman in 1915, they moved
to the house and it became a Dominion
Meteorological Office. Its landmark
status was focused on the sixty-foot red-
painted, wooden-scaffold tower mounted
on the roof that held the rotating wind
gauge. A meteorological instrument
platform was affixed to the home's rear
dormer, and others were installed in the
front room and backyard until the house
virtually bristled with instrumentation.
The devices in use included terrestrial
radiators, moisture meters, maximum
and minimum thermometers, and self-
recording rain and snow gauges.

When Herbert enlisted during the First
World War, Eda took over his duties, taking

▲   192A

daily readings from her meteorological
instruments and sending them to Toronto.
Herbert died in a prisoner-of-war camp in
1917, and Eda became the station manager,
making her the first woman to hold such a
post in Canada. Eda's daily routine began
at 5:40 a.m. with readings and telephone
reports. Over 140 weather stations
contacted her daily, and she sent two daily
and one monthly report to Toronto.

During the 1920s and 1930s, a time hungry
for unusual news, Eda's weather observatory
became a popular meeting place for
academics, exploration groups and globe-
trotting aviators passing through Edmonton.
Pressure from American military authorities
in July 1943 forced its closure during the

so-called friendly invasion of the city by U.S.
military personnel, many of whom worked
on the Northwest Staging Route, the series
of airstrips and radio-range stations built
in conjunction with the Alaska Highway.

Holgate Residence

Constructed 1912–13
6210 Ada Boulevard
Designated Provincial Historic
Resource May 1987

Though the Hudson's Bay Company and the railway companies controlled much of the land development in Western Canada, Edmonton's growth was more frequently influenced by the local business community. Bidwell Holgate was one such developer. Holgate partnered with William J. Magrath in 1909 to launch the Magrath-Holgate Company. While the company was involved in several residential subdivisions, the Highlands district would prove to be its boldest. Magrath and Holgate built their own mansions in the Highlands, hoping other prominent Edmontonians would be attracted there.

The Holgate Residence was designed by architect Ernest W. Morehouse and combined several of his favoured styles, including those embodied by the Arts and Crafts movement, which promoted the use of natural, handcrafted materials and rustic, rural English architectural influences. The suggestion of half-timbering in the interior recalls the Tudor Revival style, while the Georgian Revival style is evident in the simple, white Tuscan columns of the exterior and the oak-carved Ionic columns of the interior.

◀ 193A

GARNEAU

The Garneau neighbourhood was named for Laurent Garneau, a Métis who had taken part in the Red River Rebellion of 1870, and who settled in Edmonton in 1874 on River Lot 7 to work as a merchant. In 1901 the family moved to St. Paul.

Garneau lies between Saskatchewan Drive and University Avenue, and between 107th Street and 112th Street.

The portion of Garneau south of Whyte Avenue was once known as Strathcona Place. Unlike many of the historical districts of Edmonton, Garneau developed slowly. By 1912 there were residences along Whyte Avenue to east of 109th Street, and by the 1920s Garneau had filled in from the south and from the north.

The community has had to defend itself from high-rise development, particularly throughout the 1960s and 1970s, and now contains many University of Alberta student residences. Since the 1960s the University has purchased many historical properties, many of which were demolished in the mid-1980s. North Garneau remains under threat.

▲ *Garneau in 1944 was solidly a residential area between the University of Alberta and the heart of Strathcona.* **194A**

▲ 195A

Cecil Burgess Residence
Constructed circa 1912
10958 89th Avenue
Designated Municipal Historic
Resource July 2002

The Cecil Burgess Residence is a simple two-storey, homestead-type property with Craftsman styling featured in its timber lap-and-shingle siding and porch on the front elevation. A single-storey addition was added to the rear in 1988. The front façade, facing 89th Avenue, is characterized by its open front veranda with three columns, which rest on a solid and enclosed railing and support a hip roof, its front door located to the left of the front elevation with a small window to its upper left. There is a picture window with double-hung sidelights, one on each side, to the right of the door. The front elevation is gabled with the roof projecting and supported by five triangular knee brackets. The second floor has a centred, double-hung wooden window with small square windows located in the east and west corners. The windows all sit below a frieze board separating the second floor and gable. The ground floor is clad with clapboard and the upper floor with cedar shingles. These are separated by a timber frieze/belt course, while a timber frieze/belt course separates the main floor from the foundation.

Though the designer and builder of this house are unknown, one of the most important architects in Edmonton's history, Cecil Burgess, lived here from 1942 until 1971.

Cecil Scott Burgess was born in Bombay, India, and raised in Scotland, where he studied architecture. In 1903 he immigrated to Montreal, where he worked his profession under various principals, finally joining Percy E. Nobbs at McGill University, where he lectured. In 1913 he was invited by Dr. H. M. Tory to come to the University of Alberta to act as resident architect and "take an interest in teaching." The Department of Architecture he created and in which he served for many years as a professor was active from 1914 to 1940 and shaped a generation of local and regional architects who then would leave their mark on Edmonton. The department was active until his retirement. Cecil Burgess was responsible for the design of Pembina Hall, the staff homes on the Campus Circle, and the Arts and Medical Sciences Building.

One of the most influential early architects in Alberta, Burgess was an active member of the Edmonton Town Planning Commission and Council of the Alberta Association of Architects. He died on November 12, 1971 at the age of 101.

Sarah McLellan House

Constructed 1913
11135 84th Avenue
Designated Municipal Historic
Resource August 2001
Designated Provincial Historic
Resource June 2000

From 1916 until 1919, this property was part of the Canadian war effort, serving as a residence for nurses from the Strathcona Military Hospital which was dedicated to serving wounded, repatriated veterans. The institution later evolved into the University of Alberta Hospital.

▲ 196A

The Sarah McLellan House, located in the Garneau district, embodies the prevalent foursquare style of residential architecture of early twentieth-century residential architecture in the West. The house is associated with the establishment and development of the University of Alberta and the Garneau district. In 1907, when the Alberta Legislature passed the act providing for the creation of a provincial university, it was decided that the new campus would be laid out on the western boundary of the City of Strathcona. Two new subdivisions were created around the university site – Windsor Park and Garneau – to provide housing for students and staff.

Sarah L. McLellan was one of the earliest landowners in the Garneau district. In 1907 she purchased four lots in the area

and erected handsome residences on each. Five years later she acquired an adjacent lot and built the Sarah McClellan House as a home for herself and her husband Robert, a freighter who had worked out of Edmonton since at least 1882.

The McLellan home was completed in 1913, one year before Sarah was widowed and the city's housing market collapsed.

The home was subsequently rented by Mr. and Mrs. Royal Nickerson until 1925, at which time Mrs. Nickerson, now a widow, purchased the property from Mrs. McLellan. In the following years, the home was used as a residence for university students.

St. Joseph's Auxiliary Hospital

Constructed 1948
10722 82nd Avenue
Designated Municipal Historic Resource November 1994

St. Joseph's Auxiliary Hospital, built in 1948, is closely linked to the polio epidemics of the post-Second World War years. The upper two floors were added in 1955, and the east and west wings (auditorium and convent) were built in 1965.

This highly visible landmark on Whyte Avenue is an extremely early example of Modernist architecture in Edmonton. Although indebted to compositional principles from the Beaux Arts style, the hospital's austere design combines elements of Art Deco and International style that eliminate traditional ornament. It also features steel-frame construction with brick exterior curtain walls, an early example of the structural system that became commonplace in the 1950s.

St. Joseph's is closely associated with Most Reverend Archbishop H. J. O'Leary and the Sisters of Providence of St. Vincent de Paul. The hospital figures prominently in the medical history of the city and the province as the first institution offering chronic-care for elderly and incurable patients. In 1929 the hospital provided Edmonton's first home for the aged in

▲ 197A

the White Block (now demolished), and in 1930 it became the province's first rest home for the chronically ill. The hospital also was the first institution to make provision for the victims of the poliomyelitis epidemic of 1948. The addition of the fifth and sixth floors was intended to provide fifty beds for chronic care polio victims.

George Heath MacDonald designed this impressive structure at the height of an architectural career in Edmonton that spanned six decades. MacDonald was responsible for the design of many of the city's principal buildings. The two floors added in 1955 were designed by MacDonald's nephew and successor.

THE UNIVERSITY OF ALBERTA

The University of Alberta campus remains something of an anomaly in that it encompasses several of the more interesting and important buildings in Edmonton but remains autonomous under the University Act. It consequently consults with the City of Edmonton but is under no obligation to adhere to the wishes of municipal or heritage preservation groups. It has preserved Rutherford House, after a decisive protest saved the landmark from destruction during one of the university's expansions. Several of the Ring Houses have been destroyed, although three remain. The beautiful early halls, such as the Athabasca and Assiniboia, also have been preserved.

▲ *Athabasca Hall 198A*

◄ *Pembina Hall 198B*

Old St. Stephen's College

Constructed 1910–1911
8820 112th Street
Designated provincial historic
resource June 1983

Old St. Stephen's College is a four-storey, wood frame building located on a treed lot on the University of Alberta campus. Edmonton architect H. A. Magoon designed this striking building in the Collegiate Gothic style, a choice reflecting a trend already well established among academic institutions across North America. Magoon established an architectural precedent that would be followed on the University of Alberta campus until the advent of innovative modern forms in the 1950s.

▲ 199A

Old St. Stephen's notable architectural elements include its octagonal five-storey stairwell towers, warm red-brick veneer exterior finish, Tudor-arched main entry, fine stone detailing, crenellated parapets, tall narrow windows and wood tracery in selected windows. The college was laid out on a T-shaped plan. The first floor chapel retains its stained-glass windows, memorials and oak furnishings, while the fifth floor gymnasium boasts a large Tudor-arched window surmounting the main façade. Completing the stately scholastic atmosphere are oak entrance doors and interior details, a foyer with pilasters, plasterwork and vault, and the old dean's office with its fireplace.

Teachers gathered from around the province each year in St. Stephen's to mark the departmental examinations of Alberta high school students. One summer during the Great Depression, Calgary high-school principal William Aberhart, was among those in residence. One of his brightest students had recently committed suicide out of despair over the future. This had a profound impact on him, and he began looking for a political solution to the problems facing Alberta. While at St. Stephen's College he was introduced to Social Credit theories. He would later lead his Social Credit party to a landslide victory that would transform the province.

Old St. Stephen's College was the first building located on the grounds of Alberta's first university.

Theological students lived and studied here between 1911 and 1927. In following years it was used as a convalescent hospital, nurses' residence, army barracks, male students' residence for the university and a centre for the administration of historic sites by the Alberta Government.

GLENORA

Glenora stretches north from the North Saskatchewan River valley to 107th Avenue, and from Groat Road west to 142nd Street. The community was developed as a prestige residential neighbourhood by James Carruthers. The construction in 1909 of the bridge over Groat Ravine, which improved access to downtown and Government House, the official residence of the lieutenant-governor, reinforced that identity in the minds of Edmontonians. The "Carruthers Caveat" specified a high minimum value for all houses, ensuring that only the finest homes would be built in Glenora. The

▲ *Late 1920s aerial view of Glenora.*
200A

neighbourhood became one of the most popular locations for the professional and commercial elite who sought their own company amid its imposing dwellings. Glenora retains its original cachet to this day.

▲ 201A

Government House

Constructed 1913
12845 102nd Avenue
Designated Provincial Historic
Resource June 1985

Government House is an imposing
Edwardian sandstone mansion situated

directly south of the Royal Alberta
Museum and overlooking the North
Saskatchewan River. Government
House was the official residence
for the lieutenant-governors of
Alberta between 1913 and 1938.

Government House was the most
costly and most luxurious residence
built in Edmonton to that point, and
its design can be described as eclectic.
The exterior follows the Beaux Arts
movement, borrowing from various
historic precedents – Jacobethan

Revival features such as prominent projections, parapet gable walls and wall dormers, bay windows, battlements, and oculus openings are obvious. The exterior porches and more delicate interior details suggest the Edwardian Classical Revival style, while an Arts and Crafts influence is evident in the simplified fireplace surrounds, wainscoting, and built-in furnishings and mouldings.

Government House hosted state receptions, visiting royalty and other dignitaries, as well as many charitable and social events. In 1938 it was closed and converted to other uses, among them a military rehabilitation facility during and following the Second World War.

Lieutenant-Governor John C. Bowen, the last viceregal resident, became entangled in a serious constitutional dispute when he refused to give royal assent to three bills passed by the Alberta Legislature in 1937. Two of the bills would have placed banks under the authority of the Social Credit government of Premier William Aberhart. The third, the Accurate News and Information Act, would have forced newspapers to print government rebuttals to stories the cabinet deemed misleading. All three bills were later declared unconstitutional by the Supreme Court of Canada and the Judicial Committee of the Privy Council at Westminster, England. John C. Bowen was reappointed lieutenant-governor for a second term and continued to serve in that capacity until 1950. However, the Aberhart government decided to put Bowen out of Government House, purportedly for financial reasons.

In 1964, in anticipation of Canada's Centennial, the province reacquired and refurbished Government House as a site for state and community events.

The architect for Government House, Richard Palin Blakey, was the principal architect for Alberta Public Works from 1912 to 1923 and was responsible for many prominent public buildings. Blakey was born in Sunderland, County Durham, England, in 1879, the son of George Hudson Blakey and Mary Jane Palin Blakey. His father was a former shipwright. Blakey studied at Bede Collegiate Institute and articled with George Thomas Brown in Wales. In May 1907 he came to Canada, arriving first in Winnipeg. In June 1908 he entered the service of the provincial government of Alberta and was subsequently appointed provincial architect. An active member of Christ Church (Anglican), he and his brother, William George Blakey, also an architect, designed that church and much of its interior finishing.

Richard Blakey succeeded A. M. Jeffers as provincial architect in 1912, not long before Jeffers resigned over a controversy surrounding the management of the provincial legislature's construction. Blakey finished the Legislature Building – designing the staircase, rotunda and south wing in 1912–13 – and then turned his attention to Government House. While provincial architect, he designed many public buildings, such as courthouses and the technical schools in Calgary, Edmonton and Camrose. Blakey also was the architect responsible for Alberta's famous one-room schools, designed in 1911. He remained provincial architect until he entered into practice with R. McDowell Symonds in 1925. During 1925–26 they designed numerous schools and small hospitals across Alberta.

▲ 203A

Dr. Robert Wells Residence

Constructed 1911
10328 Connaught Drive
Designated Municipal Historic
Resource October 2002

The Wells Residence represents a modified
vernacular version of the Craftsman

style, a house-and-furniture design mode
popularized in North America during
the early twentieth century by Gustav
Stickley's magazine *The Craftsman*.

James Henderson's design is an irregular-
plan Arts and Crafts house with a

cross-gabled roof and a detached coach
house, characterized by clinker brick and
wood shingles. Henderson's work was a
notable part of the developing west end
of Edmonton, where he lived. He also
designed the C. W. Cross residence in
Glenora (1912), as well as several homes in

THE HISTORICAL AND DISTINCT DISTRICTS OF EDMONTON   203

the west end in Groat Estates. Henderson was at the peak of his architectural career when he designed the Wells Residence.

James Hay, a prominent carpenter, woodworker and contractor built the Wells Residence. He lived most of his life in Glenora and was described by the Edmonton Journal as "one of Edmonton's fine master craftsmen." Hay was born in 1872 in Carrickfergus, Northern Ireland, and came to Edmonton in 1907, where he would spend most of the remainder of his life. "Mr. Hay took part in the construction of many city public buildings," reported the Journal, "and designed and constructed or remodelled many of the city's finest homes." Hay was foreman on the construction of the first part of the Royal Alexandra Hospital and on the construction of First Presbyterian Church; he also was the contractor for the first addition to the General Hospital. While a successful contractor, Hay was equally valued as a craftsman. "Examples of his fine craftsmanship in cabinetmaking and woodworking are to be found in many of the city's public buildings," observed the Journal.

Robert Bruce Wells was born in Ontario in 1867, graduated in medicine in 1894, and after practising in India took a trip to Europe in 1903, which awakened his fascination for art. In 1906 Wells took a three-month post-graduate course in Chicago before coming to Edmonton "for climatic reasons." Dr. Wells was named president of the Edmonton Academy of Medicine in 1910. Wells joined the real estate boom and purchased his first lot the day after arriving in the city. He sold most of his property in 1910, thus avoiding the impending economic slump, and travelled with his wife to Europe. While on this extensive trip abroad in 1912, Wells purchased his first canvas. By 1929 the Edmonton Journal gave as its opinion that Dr. Wells "has perhaps one of the finest collections of oil paintings in Edmonton in his well-appointed home on the Connaught Drive."

Dr. Wells is also recalled as an active member, and sometimes chair, of the Edmonton Board of Public Welfare from 1918 to 1925, when it became inactive. During those years he was a leading figure in providing needed support for the unemployed, destitute and needy of Edmonton at a time when the postwar dislocation of the economy was felt most keenly by the poorest.

During the 1930s, Dr. Wells was a driving force in keeping the arts alive in Edmonton. He was elected president of the Edmonton Museum of Art from 1929 to 1932, and he crusaded for a permanent location for the civic collection for years. His personal collection was regularly exhibited for the enjoyment of Edmontonians.

The former Wells Pavilion at the University of Alberta Hospital was named for Dr. Robert Wells to honour his pioneering career as an eye, ear, nose and throat specialist; for some time he was a professor of ophthalmology at the University of Alberta.

WESTMOUNT

Groat Estates was an early suburban subdivision located in the Westmount community that was incorporated into the Edmonton city limits in 1912. When Edmonton was incorporated as a city in 1904, its boundaries were extended west to 127th Street. Malcolm Groat began to subdivide his substantial land holdings in the district, selling the remainder of his land to James Carruthers of Montreal in 1905. Carruthers proceeded with further subdivision, naming Westmount after the prestigious English neighbourhood in Montreal. These large estates were sold to prominent citizens who built impressive mansions on and adjacent to Villa Avenue. The John Sherry Residence is representative of the prestigious suburban enclave – sometimes referred to as Robbers' Roost in the pre-war years – where some of the city's wealthiest residents lived.

A park was developed along Groat Ravine on the western boundary of Groat Estates. Its two levels of trails proved popular for promenades and picnics.

Developers later speculated on land north of Stony Plain Road, hoping to attract young professionals to the district. The streetcar line was extended up 124th Street by 1913, making suburban development in Westmount more attractive. Villa

Avenue remains a distinctive address in a neighbourhood that retains much of its historical character. As 124th Street developed quickly into a major commercial artery, properties close to it began to fill up with dwellings. Unlike the Glenora district, the properties here were often smaller lots and the dwellings invariably wood frame. The desirability of the neighbourhood, however, attracted business people or trained professionals such as doctors, lawyers or engineers.

The merchants of the business district stretching along 124th Street between

▲ *The Edmonton Radial Railway line went north on 124th Street to the Calder area in August 1911.* **205A**

Jasper Avenue and 111th Avenue formed a business association in 1988 for the purpose of working with the City of Edmonton to stimulate growth within the business district. Many of the businesses have been on 124th Street for years. The surrounding built heritage is seen as an important part of the plan to attract people to the area.

Westmount/Inglewood was an area developed through speculation as well.

Located on the edge of Hudson's Bay Company land and railway right-of-ways, it is now also a recognized Heritage Area with its own distinctive character and landscaping, accented and identified through street signage and community entrances. Specific design guidelines in the local plan protect the existing community character. The 104th Street Heritage Area has more recently been recognized in this way.

▲ *Commercial and residential properties thrived side by side on 124th Street in 1931.* **206A**

▶ *Traffic on 124th Street in 1953 was sparser than today.* **206B**

▲ 207A

Terwillegar Residence
Constructed 1912
10727 125th Street
Designated Municipal Historic
Resource July 2004

This little Craftsman bungalow was
the home of Dr. Norman Terwillegar,
an early Edmonton surgeon and
general practitioner. He moved
with his family into this residence
in 1920, and the house remained in
the Terwillegar family until 1959.

Norman Terwillegar was born in 1884
and practised medicine in Edmonton
from 1912 until 1947. He was on the
staff of the Royal Alexandra Hospital
for over thirty-five years, and during
his career served as president of the
Edmonton Academy of Medicine, as
well as of the Alberta Division of the
Canadian Medical Association. In 1971
the Terwillegar Heights neighbourhood
was named to commemorate his
contributions to the community.

Terwillegar Park was also named for him
in 1981, as were the neighbourhoods
of Terwillegar Towne (1995) and
Terwillegar Vista (1999). Terwillegar
Drive, named in 1972, shortly after
Terwillegar Heights was developed, is
one of the most important transportation
links to the Whitemud Freeway.

▲ 208A   ▲ 208B

Charles Barker Residence

Constructed 1912
10834 125th Street
Designated Municipal Historic
Resource July 2004

This simple dwelling has weathered
the seasons in Edmonton for decades
and reminds us of typical middle-class
housing of the early twentieth century.

Its façade is characterized by the
original timber lap siding and on the
east elevation by an enclosed hip-roof
porch with two squared, slightly tapered
piers supporting the roof at either end.

Other features include a cedar-shingle roof
with two brick chimneys, a large frieze
board with simple bed moulding, exposed
projecting rafters under the eaves, a central
shed-wall dormer and exposed decorative
brackets. All timber sash windows have
simple timber surrounds and decorative
crowns. The fascia boards have a decorative
finish at the ends. On the south side is
a bay window. On the west side is a rear
porch with deck above, enclosed by a
timber lap-sided wall, an off-centre shed
dormer with a small casement window,
and a door that opens to the deck.

McIntosh Residence
(Ravina Apartments)

Constructed 1912
10325 Villa Avenue
Designated Provincial Historic
Resource August 1982

This brick mansion with its intriguingly complex roofline was built at the height of Edmonton's first construction boom by successful real estate dealer John R. McIntosh, who arrived in Edmonton in 1902. He commissioned architect Alfred Marigon Calderon, responsible for the prestigious LeMarchand Mansion, to design his home.

Graffiti discovered during an extensive renovation in 1981 indicate that G. McGlenaghan was the builder, while J. C. Sutherland was the painter and decorator.

In 1920, following the real estate crash after the First World War, the mansion was divided into seven suites by McIntosh, who had fallen on less affluent times, but who continued to live there with his wife until 1927.

McIntosh and Hugh Alfred Calder formed the Calder Land Company to subdivide the Calder farm in 1910, and it became a working-class neighbourhood located near the railway yards. He also worked as a land agent for the Hudson's Bay Company until 1946, four years before his death.

▲ 209A

The Ravina Apartments took a new name from the adjacent Groat Ravine and operated as an apartment block until 1978. It is currently a private residence.

OLIVER

Oliver stretches north of the river valley to 104th Avenue, and west of 109th Street to 124th Street. At first, this part of Edmonton was simply known as the "west end," and included Glenora, Westmount and Inglewood. Though settlement began as early as the mid-1880s, the neighbourhood's development was hampered by being physically separated from the downtown hub by about nine blocks of undeveloped land. When houses on 116th Street were completed, one resident later recalled, friends would be invited to a house-warming party. "It was considered so far out that the guests chartered a carryall to pick them up along Jasper Avenue and drive out to the country." The neighbourhood did not really grow until after 1908 when the Edmonton Radial Railway provided transit services westward. Oliver grew rapidly in the next five years before the 1913 decline in the residential market.

The neighbourhood takes its name from Frank Oliver, an influential politician involved in the struggle for status as the new Province of Alberta and the selection of Edmonton as its capital. Oliver was the founder of Edmonton's first daily newspaper, the Edmonton Bulletin. He was elected the first Alberta member of Parliament in 1905, and he sat in the House of Commons from 1896 to 1917,

during which time he was minister of the Interior and Superintendent General of Indian Affairs (1905 - 1911). Frank Oliver School was named for him in 1911 and The Oliver Community League established in 1922, probably named after the school, gave its name to the district in about 1937.

The most impressive buildings in the early days were the Church of St. Joachim (1886), the Edmonton General Hospital, a convent just south of St. Joachim, and a rectory to the north. The Misericordia Hospital (1905) and Grandin School (1914) added to what constituted a French precinct with a distinctive character reflecting the culture and history of the nearly three thousand Roman Catholics who settled in the district as early as 1885 – almost twice the combined numbers of Presbyterians, Methodists, Baptists and Church of England adherents. Prominent personalities of the time moved into Oliver, attracted to a prestigious district on the edges of the developing government precinct. Oliver's proximity to the Legislature saw Senator P. E. Lessard, Judge Lucien Dubuc, Judge N. D. Beck, Maude Bowman, first president and director of the Edmonton Museum of Art, A. Balmer Watt, editor of the Edmonton Journal, and many others take up residence here about this time.

Oliver has changed over the years. A strong Jewish community emerged in the 1930s. After the Second World War, many of the large residences were converted to apartments, and high-rise construction began to further transform Oliver during the 1960s. In 1981 the Oliver Area Redevelopment Plan was implemented to guide a balanced approach to development in a neighbourhood where many saw the encroachment of high-density housing sweeping away the built heritage in what Lawrence Herzog calls "Edmonton's earliest incarnation of suburbia".

211A

211B

Église Catholique St. Joachim

1898–1901, Renovated 1912
9920 110th Street
Designated provincial historic
resource September 1978

Église Catholique St. Joachim has been
associated with some of the most significant,
not to say legendary, early missionaries
of the Northwest in its settlement heyday.
The brick-faced frame building sits on
a solid stone foundation supported by
concrete footings. The pinnacles located
at the sides suggest the strong French-
Canadian influence in the district.

St. Joachim's parish, the oldest
Roman Catholic parish in Edmonton,
was established in 1854 by Father
Albert Lacombe. Father Lacombe
converted a tiny building inside
the walls of Fort Edmonton into a

chapel, and Bishop Alexandre Antoine
Taché later named the parish.

In 1877 Malcolm Groat donated land for a
larger church on Jasper Avenue and 121st
Street. A third church was built in 1886.
When Father Hippolyte Leduc arrived in
1896, he began to plan for a grander church.

The first service was held in December
1899, but the steeple was not completed
until 1901, and the stained-glass windows
were not finally installed until 1903. The
altar was installed in 1907, and in 1912
a sizeable vestry was attached to the
west wall. This attenuated process was
typical of churches in Edmonton at
the time and indicates the difficulty of
raising the necessary funds to realize the
grand dreams of the church members.

Robertson-Wesley United Church

Constructed 1913–14
10209 123rd Street
Designated Municipal Historic
Resource July 2004

Robertson Presbyterian Church was built in 1913 at the end of the first Edmonton building boom and opened in early 1914 on the eve of the First World War. Named for Reverend James Robertson, Superintendent of Missions for Manitoba and the Northwest Territories from 1881 to 1902, the church proudly commemorated the history of church endeavour in Western Canada.

Robertson Presbyterian became a United Church following Church Union (merging of the Presbyterian, Methodist and Congregationalists) in 1925. It joined congregations with Wesley United Church (Wesley Methodist Church before 1925) in 1971. Wesley United (117th Street and 102nd Avenue) was vacated when its congregation moved up the street to Robertson United. The church was renamed Robertson-Wesley United Church at this time.

Wesley had been active in the west end of Edmonton since 1907, and Robertson has offered ministry since 1909. Both churches were fourth in their denominations on the north side of the river. Both also reflected the phenomenal growth in their neighbourhood during the pre-war boom.

Dedicated in January 1955, the Memorial Hall and Chapel addition on the northwest corner was designed by Edmonton architect George Heath MacDonald to commemorate the war dead from both world wars. Of the congregation's 297 members who enlisted, 28 died in the service of their country, including the Rev. J. Gordon Brown, a former minister who died while serving with the Royal Canadian Air Force.

Robertson-Wesley United Church's High-Victorian Gothic-Revival style, typical of churches built before the First World War in Western Canada, was inspired directly by the design of First Baptist Church in Calgary. Constructed of Redcliff pressed brick, the building presents a front gable roof with an entry, while a bell tower with sandstone arch vents and finials soars at the southwest corner. The front doors are oak and framed in a pointed sandstone arch while the pointed arch windows are framed with sandstone tracery. The west wall is highlighted by the central stained-glass arched window with stone tracery, buttresses on either side of the central window, turrets and pediment, and the rooftop cupola.

Robertson-Wesley United Church is noted for its fine stained-glass windows. Five noteworthy practitioners of the art are represented: William N. O'Neil; Yvonne Williams and Esther Johnson; Robert McCausland; Franz Mayer and Minchin of Munich; and Winter Art Glass of Edmonton.

The oldest windows in the church are by William N. O'Neil, who was established in 1898 in Vancouver and who for some years produced commissions for Robert McCausland of Toronto, the oldest stained-glass firm in the Western Hemisphere. The windows in Robertson-Wesley carry the company signature, indicating that O'Neil produced the stained and painted glasswork. These are the only known windows by O'Neil.

A stained-glass arched window with stone tracery detailing and a pediment is featured in the east elevation. This interesting work was produced by the studio of Yvonne Williams and Esther Johnson, well-known Toronto designers and workers in stained glass, in memory of Dr. R. B. Wells, prominent Edmonton eye, ear, nose and throat specialist who died in 1940. Dr. Wells was one of the organizers of the first Mission church, which was a predecessor of Robertson Presbyterian Church. He suggested naming the church to honour James Robertson, Presbyterian missionary superintendent for the Northwest Territories from 1881 to 1902. He was an elder at Robertson from

its inception until his death. His Glenora residence is a municipal historical resource. The memorial window in Robertson-Wesley was installed by his widow in 1941.

◄ 213A

Westminster Apartments
Constructed 1912–13
9955 114th Street
Designated Municipal Historic
Resource December 2002

Westminster Apartments was a classically styled L-shaped building clad on its two principal elevations with a distinctive red-brown wire-cut brick. The textured finish of the brick is accented with decorative corbelling and repetitive horizontal rustication banding extending from the foundation line to the course separating the first and second floors. Brick corbelling and detail tile work can also be seen on the chimney projections at the roof level at the east end of the building. A deeply projecting painted metal cornice with decorative flower rosettes enhances the classical statement. The Westminster façade also features distinctive glazed-porcelain accent tiles. The use of contrasting glazed tiles and bricks as a major decorative element is similar to design themes seen in Edmonton in the H. V. Shaw Building (1914), the Gibson Block (1913), the Salvation Army Citadel (1925) and Schwermann Hall (1926) at Concordia College.

Western Canada Properties Ltd., a land development company headed by Robert B. Scott and H. T. Tilley and financed with central Canadian capital, built the Westminster Apartments in 1912. The company likely purchased

▲ 214A

blueprints for a standard apartment building from an architectural firm rather than retaining a specific architect. The company also apparently acted as its own general contractor. The apartments continue to operate as living units, though now as private condo units.

215A ▶

GLOSSARY OF ARCHITECTURAL TERMS

Arcading: A row of arches supported on columns carved in relief as decoration on a solid wall.

Arts and Crafts Movement: An English design movement originating in the nineteenth century, based on traditional English forms which emphasized craftsmanship and organic design shapes.

Balustrade: A row of balusters supporting a stairway handrail, or sometimes a series of balusters between pedestals or cornices, forming a kind of parapet. A baluster is any upright support in a balustrade, either round, square, turned or an ornamented bar or rod.

Banding: A band is a flat, raised horizontal strip located on a façade, sometimes simply ornamental, or corresponding with sills or floor levels. Sometimes called a banding belt, belt course, or any of many other terms.

Bay: A regular structural subdivision of a building, or part of a framed building between the main supporting timbers.

Bay Window: A window placed in an angular projection of the wall beyond its general structural line. A bay window on an upper floor only is called an oriel.

Beaux-Arts Classicism: A style taught at the École des Beaux-Arts in Paris in the nineteenth century, based on an eclectic mixture of historic classical elements.

Bell-cast Roof: A roof with eaves which flare out.

Boom-town Front Architecture: A false front which hides the actual roofline, intended to increase the apparent size and dignity of frontier commercial architecture. Ornament is usually classical in origin. Overhanging cornices and round arched windows are common features.

Buttress: An exterior, attached pier intended to reinforce a wall.

Cantilever: A horizontal structural element projecting from a wall without support at any point within its entire projection, but capable of carrying loads, and prevented from falling by means of a heavy structural deadweight at the other end of the projection.

Chicago School: A commercial style of architecture pioneered in Chicago in the late nineteenth century, used especially in tall buildings and characterized by steel or iron-frame construction and triple-paned Chicago windows.

Clapboard: The overlapping and wedge-shaped horizontal boards which cover a wood-frame wall.

Clinker Brick: Brick that has been over-fired to produce a distinctive textured surface.

Cogging: A course of projecting bricks laid diagonally to give a sawtooth effect in a cornice or belting-course.

Commercial Style: Refers to a type of late-nineteenth-century to early-twentieth-century commercial building which is generally five to sixteen storeys high. The character of their façades derives from the fenestration and ornamentation, which, when present, is usually limited to the cornice and ground level.

Corbelling: A projection or series of stepped projections in masonry and especially in brick. A corbel is a projection from the face of a wall, characterized by a block built into the wall, supporting an arch, beam, parapet, or truss. Corbelling consists of successive courses of corbels forming a "pseudo-vault" or supporting an element projecting over the wall below.

Corinthian Column: The most slender and ornate classical order. The Corinthian Order usually has a fluted shaft with leaf and scroll shapes in the capital.

Cornice: Any projecting decorative moulding along the top of a building, wall, or arch. Course: Any horizontal, level range of bricks or stones placed according to some rule or order in the construction of a wall, and laid evenly.

Crenellation: A wall notched or indented at the top. Crenels are part of a battlement parapet, and describe the indentations located between the higher, tooth-like parts.

Cross Gable: A gable parallel to the roof ridge on the main part of a building.

Cupola: Generally used to describe a dome-shaped roof on a round base, often surmounting another dome.

Curtain Wall: In modern construction, this refers to a thin subsidiary wall between piers or other structural components. The curtain consists of a "filling," which does not support other parts of the building. Entire non-load-bearing skins on buildings, usually made of metal or glass cladding, have become a hallmark of modern construction.

Dentilation: Consists of an arrangement of dentils, or "toothing." Dentils are blocks forming a long series set closely together under a cornice.

Doric Column: A column of the classical Greek Doric order. The column may be smooth or fluted, the capital and base are of the simple cushion type.

Dormer: A window placed vertically in a sloping roof with a roof of its own.

Double-hung window: A two-part window in which the counter-weighted panes slide up and down in the frame, also called a sash window.

Elevation: In general usage, any external façade.

Entablature: The entire horizontal mass of material supported by columns and pilasters.

Façade: The exterior face or wall of a building.

Fenestration: A pattern formed by windows in a façade.

Finial: An ornament which is situated at the point of a spire or at the end of a gable.

Foursquare Style: Derived from Georgian Colonial sources, the foursquare residence is square in plan, usually one-and-a-half to two-and-a-half storeys capped by a pyramidal or hipped roof. Ornamentation is classical in nature, but is used more sparingly than in Georgian Revival designs.

Frieze: A horizontal central band of a classical entablature below the cornice.

Gable: A vertically triangular portion of the end of a building having a double sloping roof, hence, gable roof. See Cross Gable.

Georgian Revival: The nineteenth- and twentieth-century revival of eighteenth-century English architecture derived from classical, Renaissance and Baroque forms.

Gothic Arch: Any arch with a point at its apex, characteristic of, but not confined to, Gothic architecture.

Gothic Revival: The nineteenth-century revival of medieval architecture characterized by pointed arches and complex ornamentation, including crockets, finials, gingerbread trim, and high-pitched roofs.

Half-timbering: Exposed timber foundations, supports, etc., the walls of which are filled in with plaster or other materials.

High-Victorian Gothic Revival: A middle phase of the Gothic Revival, characterized by polychromatic ornament and an abundance of heavy, architectural detailing.

Hipped Roof: A roof sloped on all four sides; the sides meet at a centre ridge.

Ionic Column: A column of the classical Ionic order, usually fluted, with large scroll-shaped capitals.

Jacobethan Revival: A term coined in 1933 for the nineteenth-century revival of later sixteenth-century Elizabethan and early seventeenth-century Jacobean English architecture which combined Gothic and Renaissance elements.

Keystone: In masonry, the central, often embellished, voussoir of an arch. Until the keystone is in place, no true arch action is incurred.

Late Gothic Revival Style: The last of three phases of the Gothic Revival. It is distinguished from the High-Victorian Gothic Revival in that the use of Gothic motifs is less emphatic.

Lintel: Beam over an aperture which carries the wall above and spans the space between jambs or columns.

Mansard Roof: A roof having a double slope on all four sides. The lower slope is longer and steeper than the upper.

Moderne Style: A style popularized in the 1920s to 1940s characterized by curved corners, strip windows, large unrelieved surfaces, and a generally streamlined appearance.

Mullion: A vertical post placed between the lights of a window or screen.

Newel Post: A continuous vertical component which forms the axis of a circular stair, or any upright member set at a turning point of a stair.

Niche: A wall recess intended to hold a sculpture or other decorative element.

Oculus Window: A rounded or circular aperture in a wall.

Palladian Motif: A door or window in three parts, separated by posts, the two outer being flat-topped, and the central higher and arched.

Parapet: A low wall along the edge of a roof which may be crenellated or otherwise embellished.

Pediment: The triangular gable end extending from the roof above the cornice which is often highly decorated. This element may also be found over a window or door.

Pier: A column or mass of masonry attached to a wall designed to support a concentrated load.

Pilaster: A shallow pier or pillar projecting only slightly from a wall.

Porte Cochère: Doorway to a house or courtyard to allow wheeled vehicles to enter from the street. Consequently, they are built on a grand scale.

Portico: A covered or roofed space at the entrance of a building. In a classical portico, the roof pediment is supported by columns.

Post-and-sill construction: A type of wood construction characterized by horizontal beams slotted into vertical posts.

Pratt Truss: Bridge trusses identified by their diagonal members, which all slant downward and inward toward the centre of the span, with the exception of those on the ends. All the diagonal members are subject to tension forces, while the shorter vertical members handle the compressive forces. Pratt trusses are used on longer spans than are permitted by Warren trusses.

Provincial Historic Resource: A building of considerable historic and/or architectural significance to the province. Because of its importance, alteration to the structure requires the approval of the Minister of Alberta Culture and Multiculturalism.

Queen Anne Style: A style of architecture employed in Canada between the 1870s and circa 1915, which was based on Elizabethan country-home and cottage architecture.

Quoin: Stones or brickwork located at the corners of a building usually employed as decorations or for reinforcing the external corner or edge of a wall.

Registered Historic Resource: A building which is deemed to be of importance in terms of historical and/or architectural evolution of the province. The Minister of Alberta Culture and Multiculturalism must be notified ninety days in advance of effecting any changes to the building.

Renaissance Revival Style: The nineteenth- and early-twentieth-and sixteenth-century architectural styles and motifs, most often as these occurred in Italy. This style is characterized by classical orders, round arches, and symmetrical composition.

Reveal: A vertical return, or side of a wall aperture, and the plain surface of that wall. A return is simply a part of a building that turns at an angle from its principal face.

Rustication: A type of masonry in which the stone is cut so the joints are sunk in a channel, with the faces of the stones projecting beyond the channels. The faces are usually roughened to form a contrast with the dressed ashlar surrounding it.

Soffit: The visible underside of any architectural feature such as an arch, cornice or vault.

Tapestry Brick: Brick which has at least one roughened face, used for facing work.

Terra Cotta: Hard unglazed fired clay used for ornamental detail work and floor and roof tile.

Transom: A horizontal bar separating a door from the window above it. A transom light is a window above a transom bar.

Tudor Revival: The nineteenth- and twentieth-century revival of English architecture of the early sixteenth century characterized by low pointed arches called Tudor arches.

Turret: A small tower, often cantilevered.

Tuscan Column: The simplest of the classical orders, with a plain base and simple cap.

Tyndall Stone: Dolomitic limestone quarried near Garson, Manitoba. It is pale cream, with mottling caused by marine creatures which burrowed into the limestone as it was deposited. Its first use in building was in Lower Fort Garry, Manitoba, in 1832. At this time, the stone was shipped from the railway at Tyndall, Manitoba, giving it the name Tyndall Stone.

Ukrainian-Canadian Church Style: A church style imported from Ukraine which evolved from tenth- and eleventh-century Byzantine and seventeenth-century Baroque architectural traditions.

Veneer: A decorative facing with no structural function. Brick and terra cotta are typical veneers.

Voussoir: Stone, brick or terra cotta block, shaped on the two opposite long sides to a converging plane so that it forms a somewhat wedge-like shape. It forms part of the arch or vault.

Wainscoting: Fine wooden wall panelling. In the United States it may also be referred to as a timber dado.

Warren Truss: One of the most common bridge trusses, used for simple and continuous trusses. No vertical members are used in the shortest spans, giving this structure a very simple look.

Ken Tingley

Ken Tingley has been a public historian in Edmonton, Alberta, since the early 1970s. Initially involved in the local history scene as a researcher at Edmonton's historic Fort Edmonton Park, Ken later became an active participant in and supporter of the Edmonton Historical Board, local museums and various heritage groups.

He has authored, researched and edited numerous publications. Recent books include *Ride of the Century: the Story of the Edmonton Transit System; Last Best West: Glimpses of the Prairie Provinces from the Golden Age of Postcards; Recalling the Buffalo: The Martin S. Garretson Collection; The Calgary Stampede: A Collection of Vintage Postcards; My Heart's in the Highlands: The Building of a Historic Edmonton Community* and *Alberta Remembers: Recalling Our Rural Roots* for the province of Alberta's Centennial.

In 2012, Edmonton made history in selecting Ken Tingley as the first municipal Historian Laureate in Canada.

Lawrence Herzog

Lawrence Herzog was born and raised in Edmonton and has been photographing and writing about the city's history and heritage for more than 25 years. Lawrence is the author of two Edmonton community history books and his columns on heritage issues appeared in *Real Estate Weekly* from 1991 to 2011. He now tells the stories of historic Edmonton buildings on the Edmonton Heritage Council's website at www.edmontonheritage.ca

Lawrence has served as a member of the Edmonton Historical Board, and has chaired the city's Historic Resources Review Panel.

PHOTO CREDITS

Cover

Front Cover: Lawrence Herzog, High Level Bridge and McLeod Block detail.

Inside Flap Front: Lawrence Herzog, Gibson Block.

Inside Flap Back: Lawrence Herzog, Hull Block.

Back Cover: Lawrence Herzog, Foote House, Goodridge Block and Balfour Manor.

Pages

Title page: Lawrence Herzog, High Level Bridge.

04A: Lawrence Herzog, Strathcona Fire Hall #1.

1A: Lawrence Herzog, Goodridge Block.

1: City of Edmonton, Mayor Mandel.

2A: Lawrence Herzog, Muttart Conservatory.

2B: Lawrence Herzog, Knox Presbyterian Church.

3A: Lawrence Herzog, Ritchie Mill.

3B: Lawrence Herzog, Ward Residence.

4A: Jim Dobie, Connaught Armoury.

6A: City of Edmonton, aerial image of Edmonton.

8A: Lawrence Herzog, High Level Bridge.

9A: City of Edmonton Archives, ea-160-165.

9B: City of Edmonton Archives, eb-14-31.

10A: City of Edmonton Archives, ea-413-3.

11A: HBC Archives, pam 1987/363-S-25/T78 (N13855).

11B: City of Edmonton Archives, ea-9-327.

12A: Paul Kane, oil painting, title 'Fort Edmonton', Royal Ontario Museum.

14A: City of Edmonton Archives, ea-10-94.

15A: City of Edmonton Archives, ea-58-3.

16A: City of Edmonton Archives, ea-190-7.

17A: City of Edmonton Archives, ea -160-1405.

18A: City of Edmonton Archives, ea-10-1369.

20A: City of Edmonton Archives, ea- 10-269.

20B: City of Edmonton Archives, ea- 10-2929.

21A: Provincial Archives of Alberta, B783.

21B: City of Edmonton Archives, ea- 17-8.

22A: City of Edmonton Archives, ea- 10-3216.

23A: City of Edmonton Archives, ea-10-247.

23B: City of Edmonton Archives, ea-500-353.

24A: Lawrence Herzog, Strathcona Hotel.

25A: City of Edmonton, John Walter House.

25B: City of Edmonton, John Walter Houses.

26A: Lawrence Herzog, John Walter Houses.

26B: Lawrence Herzog, John Walter Houses.

27A: Lawrence Herzog, Orange Hall.

28A: Lawrence Herzog, Pendennis Hotel.

29A: City of Edmonton Archives, ea-163-87.

30A: City of Edmonton Archives, ea -10-203.

32A: City of Edmonton Archives, ea -50-03.

32B: City of Edmonton Archives, ea -24-15.

33A: City of Edmonton Archives, ea -122-121.

33B: Provincial Archives of Alberta, A5629.

34A: Lawrence Herzog, McDougal Church.

35A: City of Edmonton Archives, ea -10-668.

35B: City of Edmonton Archives, ea -256-06.

35C: City of Edmonton Archives, ea –10-2326.

36A: City of Edmonton Archives, ea -267-244.

36B: City of Edmonton Archives, ea -500-322.

37A: Lawrence Herzog, McKay School.

38A: Lawrence Herzog, CPR Station.

38B: Lawrence Herzog, CPR Station.

39A: Lawrence Herzog, Margaret Martin Residence.

40A: Lawrence Herzog, Jasper Block.

41A: Lawrence Herzog, Union Bank.

42A: City of Edmonton Archives, ea -10-222.

43A: Lawrence Herzog, LeMarchand Mansion.

44A: City of Edmonton Archives, ea -270-16.

45A: Lawrence Herzog, Carter Residence.

45B: City of Edmonton, Carter Barn.

46A: Lawrence Herzog, Hugh Duncan Residence.

46B: Lawrence Herzog, Hugh Duncan Residence.

47A: Lawrence Herzog, High Level Bridge.

48A: City of Edmonton Archives, ea -24-11.

48B: Lawrence Herzog, High Level Bridge and Trolley.

49A: Lawrence Herzog, Thomas Scott Residence.

50A: Lawrence Herzog, North Telephone Building.

51A: Lawrence Herzog,
North Telephone Building.

52A: Lawrence Herzog,
First Presbyterian Church.

53A: Lawrence Herzog,
First Presbyterian Church.

54A: Lawrence Herzog,
Molstad Residence.

55A: Lawrence Herzog,
George Durrand Residence.

56A: Lawrence Herzog,
Sheriff Robertson Residence.

57A: Lawrence Herzog, Gibson Block.

58A: Lawrence Herzog,
A. MacDonald Building.

60A: Jim Dobie,
Holy Trinity Anglican Church.

61A: Lawrence Herzog,
Strathcona Post Office.

62A: City of Edmonton Archives, ea -10-804.

64A: City of Edmonton Archives, ea -24-15.

64B: City of Edmonton Archives, ea -24-29.

65A: City of Edmonton Archives, ea -10-880.

65B: City of Edmonton Archives, ea -297-12.

65C: Provincial Archives of Alberta, A4838.

66A: City of Edmonton Archives, ea -362-69.

67A: Lawrence Herzog,
Prince of Wales Armories.

68A: Lawrence Herzog,
Prince of Wales Armories.

69A: Lawrence Herzog,
Canada Permanent Building.

69B: Lawrence Herzog,
Canada Permanent Building.

70A: Provincial Archives of Alberta A95-187.

71A: Lawrence Herzog, Metals Building.

71B: Lawrence Herzog, Metals Building.

72A: Lawrence Herzog, Princess Theatre.

73A: Lawrence Herzog, Princess Theatre.

74A: Lawrence Herzog, Princess Theatre.

75A: City of Edmonton, Hagmann Block.

75B: Calgary Glenbow Archives, nc-6-747.

76A: Lawrence Herzog, McLeod Block.

77A: Lawrence Herzog, Shaw Block.

78A: Lawrence Herzog, Shaw Block.

79A: Lawrence Herzog, Hecla Block.

80A: City of Edmonton Archives, ea -10-152.

82A: City of Edmonton Archives, ea -662-10.

83A: Lawrence Herzog,
Emily Murphy Residence.

84A: Lawrence Herzog, Bentley Farm.

85A: Lawrence Herzog, Trudel House.

86A: Lawrence Herzog, Ernest Brown Block.

87A: Lawrence Herzog, Ernest Brown Block.

88A: Lawrence Herzog, Ernest Brown Block.

89A: City of Edmonton Archives, ea -3676.

90A: Jim Dobie, McTarggart Residence.

91A: Provincial Archives of Alberta, a10641.

92A: City of Edmonton Archives, ea -662-12.

94A: City of Edmonton Archives, ea -514-6.

95A: City of Edmonton, Immigration Hall.

96A: City of Edmonton, Immigration Hall.

97A: Lawrence Herzog,
Oblates Maison Provinciale.

98A: Jim Dobie, Balfour.

99A: Jim Dobie, Chandler Barn.

100A: Lawrence Herzog,
Goodridge Block.

102A: City of Edmonton Archives,
ea -20-7273.

104A: City of Edmonton Archives,
ea -10-3181.58.1.

105A: City of Edmonton Archives, ea -174-8.

106A: City of Edmonton Archives,
ea -3181-57-1.

106B: City of Edmonton Archives,
ea 267-145.

107A: Jim Dobie, Hanger 14.

108A: Lawrence Herzog, Hanger 14.

109A: Jim Dobie, Hudson Bay
Building / Enterprise Square.

110A: Jim Dobie, Garneau Theatre.

111A: Jim Dobie, Arndt's Machine Shop.

111B: Jim Dobie, Arndt's Machine Shop.

112A: City of Edmonton Archives, ea -10-359.

114A: City of Edmonton Archives, ea -331-02.

115A: City of Edmonton Archives,
ea -10-1041.

116A: Lawrence Herzog, Hyndman House.

117A: Lawrence Herzog,
Blakely Residence.

118A: Lawrence Herzog,
Churchill Wire Centre.

119A: Lawrence Herzog,
Churchill Wire Centre.

119B: Lawrence Herzog,
Churchill Wire Centre.

120A: James Dow, World Trade Centre.

121A: Lawrence Herzog, Phillips Building.

122A: Lawrence Herzog,
St. Francis of Assisi Friary.

123A: Lawrence Herzog,
St. Francis of Assisi Friary.

124A: Lawrence Herzog,
Richard Wallace Residence.

125A: Lawrence Herzog,
Richard Wallace Residence.

126A: City of Edmonton Archives, et-17-50.

128A: James Dow,
Queen Elizabeth Planetarium.

128B: City of Edmonton Archives, et-17-113.

129A: City of Edmonton Archives, et-17-4.

129B: City of Edmonton Archives, et-17-3.

130A: Jim Dobie, Valley View Manor.

131A: Jim Dobie, Valley View Manor.

132A: City of Edmonton Archives, ea-340-56.

134A: City of Edmonton Archives, et-17-66.

135A: City of Edmonton Archives,
eb-28-1612.

135B: City of Edmonton Archives, ea -270-14.

136A: Lawrence Herzog,
Magrath Mansion.

136B: Lawrence Herzog,
Magrath Mansion

137A: Lawrence Herzog,
Rutherford House

138A: City of Edmonton Archives,
ea -340-2012.

140A: James Dow, Peter Hemingway pool.

141A: City of Edmonton Archives,
ea -340-2041.

141B: Jim Dobie, Space Science Centre.

142A: Lawrence Herzog, Grant McEwan.

144A: Jim Dobie, Alberta Art Gallery.

145A: City of Edmonton, City Hall.

146A: Lawrence Herzog,
Hotel MacDonald.

146B: Lawrence Herzog,
Hotel MacDonald

147A: Lawrence Herzog,
Kingston Powell Building.

147B: Lawrence Herzog,
Kingston Powell Building.

148A: Lawrence Herzog, Hull Block.

149A: Lawrence Herzog,
Roy Gerolamy Residence.

149B: Lawrence Herzog,
Roy Gerolamy Residence.

150A: City of Edmonton, skyline.

152A: City of Edmonton Archives, ea -64-8.

153A: City of Edmonton, Aerial shot.

155A: Jim Dobie, Canadian
Consolidated Rubber Co. Building.

156A: City of Edmonton Archives,
ea -20-113.

158A: City of Edmonton Archives,
ea -10-272.

160A: Lawrence Herzog,
Strathcona Fire Hall 1.

161A: City of Edmonton Archives,
ea -20-100.

162A: Lawrence Herzog, Strathcona Library.

163A: Lawrence Herzog, Strathcona Library.

164A: Lawrence Herzog, Gainer Block.

165A: Lawrence Herzog, Gainer Block.

166A: Lawrence Herzog, Duggan Residence.

167A: Lawrence Herzog, Duggan Residence.

168A: Lawrence Herzog, Sheppard Residence.

169A: Jim Dobie, Douglas Block.

171A: Jim Dobie, Connaught Armoury.

172A: Lawrence Herzog, Bard Residence.

173A: City of Edmonton Archives,
ea -160-1354.

174A: Lawrence Herzog, Rossdale Brewery.

175A: Lawrence Herzog, Ross Flats.

176A: Lawrence Herzog,
Hudson Bay Company Stables

177A: Lawrence Herzog,
Rossdale Power Plant.

178A: Lawrence Herzog, Foote House.

179A: Lawrence Herzog,
Parkview Apartments.

180A: City of Edmonton Archives,
McCauley aerial.

181A: Lawrence Herzog,
St. Josaphat Cathedral.

181B: Lawrence Herzog,
St. Josaphat Cathedral.

182A: Lawrence Herzog,
St. Josaphat Cathedral.

183A: Lawrence Herzog,
Rehwinkel Parsonage.

184A: City of Edmonton Archives,
ea -267-331.

185A: Lawrence Herzog, Lambton Block.

185B: City of Edmonton Archives,
ea -10-1993.

186A: City of Edmonton Archives,
ea -10-246.

187A: Jim Dobie, Canadian
Consolidated Rubber Co. Building.

188A: Lawrence Herzog, Canadian
Consolidated Rubber Co. Building.

189A: Lawrence Herzog, Armstrong Block.

190A: Lawrence Herzog,
    Armstrong Block.

190B: City of Edmonton Archives,
    ea -778-226.

191A: City of Edmonton Archives,
    ea -500-247.

191B: Lawrence Herzog,
    Magrath Mansion.

192A: Lawrence Herzog,
    Eda Owen Residence.

193A: Lawrence Herzog,
    Holgate Residence.

194A: City of Edmonton Archives,
    ea -160-292.

195A: Lawrence Herzog,
    Cecil Burgess House.

196A: Lawrence Herzog,
    Sarah McLellan Residence.

197A: Lawrence Herzog,
    St. Joseph's Hospital.

198A: Lawrence Herzog, Athabasca Hall.

198B: Lawrence Herzog, Pembina Hall

199A: Lawrence Herzog,
    St. Stephens College.

201A: Lawrence Herzog, Government House.

203A: Lawrence Herzog,
    Dr. Robert Wells Residence.

205A: City of Edmonton Archives,
    ea -246-51.

206A: Provincial Archives of Alberta, B4782.

206B: Provincial Archives of Alberta, A11716.

207A: Jim Dobie, Terwillegar Residence.

208A: Lawrence Herzog,
Charles Barker Residence.

208B: Lawrence Herzog,
    Charles Barker Residence.

209A: Lawrence Herzog,
    McIntosh Residence.

211A: Lawrence Herzog, St. Joachim.

211B: Lawrence Herzog, St. Joachim.

213A: Lawrence Herzog, Roberson Wesley.

214A: Lawrence Herzog,
    Westminster Apartments

215A: Lawrence Herzog,
    Westminster Apartments

221: Ken Tingley, Lawrence Herzog.

INDEX